Rohit Ghai

TARKARI

An Hachette UK Company
www.hachette.co.uk

First published in Great Britain
in 2021 by Kyle Books, an imprint
of Octopus Publishing Group Limited

Carmelite House
50 Victoria Embankment
London EC4Y 0DZ
www.kylebooks.co.uk

ISBN: 978 0 85783 932 9

Distributed in the US by Hachette Book Group,
1290 Avenue of the Americas, 4th and 5th Floors,
New York, NY 10104

Distributed in Canada by Canadian Manda Group,
664 Annette St., Toronto, Ontario, Canada M6S 2C8

Publisher: Jo Copestick
Publishing Director: Judith Hannam
Senior Commissioning Editor: Louise McKeever
Design: Evi-O.Studio | Susan Le and Zoe Gojnich
Photography: Maja Smend
Food Stylist: Rosie Reynolds
Prop Stylist: Lydia McPherson
Food Assistant: Sonali Shah
Production: Katherine Hockley

A Cataloguing in Publication record for this title
is available from the British Library

Printed and bound in China

10 9 8 7 6 5 4 3 2 1

I would like to dedicate
TARKARI to my father,
Mr. G. D. Ghai, who left us
on the 6th May 2020.

TARKARI

Vegetarian and Vegan
Indian Dishes
with Heart and Soul

PHOTOGRAPHY BY
MAJA SMEND

KYLE BOOKS

CONTENTS

Nashta

**BREAKFAST
AND SNACKS**

22

Rassa

CURRIES

86

Chakna

**SMALL SHARING
PLATES**

52

Dal &
Sabzi

SIDE DISHES

120

INTRODUCTION

6

THE MAGIC OF SPICES

10

MY SPICE BLENDS

16

Roti & Chawal

RICE AND BREADS

144

Meetha

DESSERTS

180

Achar & Chutney

PICKLES AND DIPS

166

Rohit's Feasting Menus

196

INDEX
202

GLOSSARY
205

THANK YOU NOTE
208

One of my mother's favourite sayings is, 'If you cook with your heart and soul, you don't need special ingredients.' I am the youngest in my family, so I was the one who spent the most time with her, watching her cook and learning her techniques, and then, as I grew older, helping her prepare meals for the family. The food that I cook in my restaurants has always been influenced by my mother, so when I was asked to write this book, I wanted to dedicate it to her. These recipes are inspired by her ideas and what I learned from her.

Tarkari is a very common term in India. A Bengali word, it refers to any vegetable dish and is used across South Asia – in Bangladesh, Nepal and Pakistan, too. It covers curries, stir-fries and side dishes, everything from the simple to the complicated. Most of Punjab in northern India, where I come from, is not vegetarian, but my family is. My favourite dish from childhood is the Punjabi cornflour flatbread makki ki roti, a seasonal dish traditionally made when it's cold and eaten with mustard leaf saag bhaji and rajmal chawal, a northern Indian dish of kidney beans and rice. If I am lucky enough to be able to visit in winter, my mother will make makki ki roti for me, along with her bottlegourd dumplings and khichadi. Khichadi is another very traditional, home-style dish of rice and lentils. It is not usually found on restaurant menus, but at my restaurant Kutir I give it a little stardust by adding truffles. In this book, I have given it my own home-cooking twist – using wild mushrooms, which impart a wonderfully earthy flavour. This is something I also want to demonstrate here. Indian food is often thought to be overly complicated, with lengthy recipes, but the tasty vegetarian dishes that we cook at home are often very simple.

They are also flexible and adapt easily to where you are and to the seasons. If you can't get hold of bottlegourd, you can use courgettes. Only white button mushrooms are available, in India, but in the UK I use all kinds – shiitake, girolles and chestnuts. Aubergines are a large part of Indian cooking and are now very popular here, too. I love them, especially in the Punjabi dish baingan ka bharta, where you take the whole aubergine and grill it over a slow fire or in a tandoor, then remove the skin and cook the pulp with green chillies and fresh peas. Cauliflower, too, is given great flavour in Indian cooking – think of the famous aloo gobi.

I believe Indian cooking also suits vegan food very well. Vegan curries offer so much, with their combinations of spices cooked with onions and tomatoes – the variations are endless. Northern Indian food uses a lot of butter and ghee, but now that so many people are more health-conscious, we are starting to use dairy alternatives, such as rapeseed oil and soy butter and yoghurt. I don't really use coconut milk in my cooking because its strong flavour is more suited to southern Indian dishes.

It was not my plan to become a professional chef but, after I finished school, I studied Hotel Management at the Institute of Culinary Management in Gwalior, which is affiliated with Pusa University in New Delhi. I then trained at two of the biggest hotel groups in India – the Taj Hotel and Resort Group and the Oberoi Hotel Group. I wanted international exposure, so when I was asked to lead Michelin-starred kitchens in London I jumped at the chance. I opened my own restaurant, Kutir, in 2018, then KoolCha, with my third restaurant set to open late 2021.

I always consider four key elements when I am cooking both in my restaurant and my home:

BALANCE

It is essential to balance the flavours of your ingredients and spices while cooking. Always taste and adjust as you cook. The perfect combination makes for the perfect dish.

TEXTURE

Texture makes the dish visually appealing as well as mouth-wateringly delicious. Having a couple of different textures in a dish – crispy and crunchy or smooth and silky – will enhance the appeal significantly.

COLOUR

If your dish looks appetising, it will awake your taste buds. I always try to pair complementary or unusual natural colours in my dishes to make them look sensational. An easy way to do this, is by adding dollops of colourful and vibrant dips and sauces.

CONSISTENCY

Execution is as important in the home as it is in the restaurant. Even if you have limited space and equipment, if you buy the best-quality ingredients, prep them as necessary and read the recipe through first, you can make quick and easy dishes consistently.

As this is my first cookbook, I am going back to my roots. In Punjab, we tend to have heavy breakfasts and lighter lunches, so my first chapter focuses on breakfast dishes such as stuffed parathas, but you can also eat them as a substantial brunch or as a snack or light meal. Subsequent chapters cover sharing plates and Indian-style salads, many of which are my own invention as I give traditional recipes a fresh and lighter twist. Then there are curries and accompanying side dishes. I give vegan options for many of my vegetarian dishes. Indian desserts are often milk-based, but I have chosen a few of my favourite fruit-based ones, too.

And then I have created my Feast menus. At Kutir, I want my guests to feel as if they are enjoying something special, so we offer tasting menus. For this book, I wanted to create something for you to prepare at home for a special occasion or when you entertain.

My finishing thought is for my mother. She avoids all ready-made foods and makes her garam masala with a mortar and pestle rather than an electric grinder because that affects the flavour. I want you to learn about the magic of spices and what a difference it makes when you use whole spices instead of pre-ground.

The Magic of Spices

Spices play a major role in Indian cooking, bringing layers of flavour, colour and texture to food, so it's no surprise that India is both the biggest producer and consumer of spices. I see them as magical ingredients that can transform a simple dish into something more complex and interesting with very little effort. This is especially true for vegan and vegetarian food, as spices can replace the nuances of taste that meat, fish and dairy bring to dishes.

Beyond their culinary use, spices also have medicinal value – we use cumin and carom seeds to help digestion. Fennel seeds are taken with a glass of just-boiled water to soothe the stomach, and turmeric has many health benefits – I find it an effective antiseptic.

Like so many things, I first learned how to use spices in my mother's kitchen. Her spice mixes, hand blended of course, form the basis of her cooking. Now I grind and blend all my spices for my restaurants, and I am launching my own range, The Magic of Spices, because I want to show you how to use them in your Indian cooking.

Spices will age and lose their flavour over time, but whole spices will last longer than ground ones. Ground will usually keep for 4–6 months and whole for 12 months if kept in airtight containers, somewhere cool and dry, away from direct sunlight. I strongly advise you, therefore, to buy your spices whole and grind them at home in smaller quantities as needed. What follows is a guide to the spices I use most often.

MY SPICE RACK

These are the spices you should always have to hand. They play a hugely important role in all my kitchens, both at home and in my restaurants. Curry powder is, of course, very popular and is an easy way for those new to cooking Indian food to create our classic flavours, but I think of it as a blend of our most important spices – cumin, coriander, turmeric, cayenne chilli, Kashmiri chilli, black peppercorns, fennel and mustard seeds.

CARDAMOM

(1) I use whole pods of green cardamom, but if you prefer you can remove the outer casing and just crush the aromatic seeds. Black cardamom isn't often used, but I like it and use it both whole and as seeds. It has a strong smell and a unique flavour.

CINNAMON

(2) One of the most important ingredients in spice mixes such as garam masala, cinnamon is used both whole and ground and is added to savoury and sweet dishes as well as to drinks. I use it to flavour a kulfi that accompanies my chocolate lawa cake, which really works well.

CLOVES

(3) Used whole or ground, cloves are strong in flavour, so you don't need very many. They are a key spice in garam masala and are also found in sweet dishes.

CORIANDER SEEDS

(4) These give a curry body and smoothness and are also good for digestion. Also used ground, coriander often goes hand in hand with cumin.

CUMIN SEEDS

(5) Good for health and digestion, cumin is the most important spice in Indian cooking. It has an earthy aroma with a little bitterness, and is used both whole and ground. Whole seeds can be roasted and used to finish dishes – cumin is often used for tempering (see page 21).

KALPASI (BLACK STONE FLOWER)

(6) Called patthar ke phool in India, this spice is used in meat dishes and biryani as well in as vegetarian dishes. A key spice in many of my spice blends, including garam masala, Chettinad spice mix and goda masala, as well as in awadhi food from northern India. It brings a distinctive black colour as well as an earthy flavour.

KASHMIRI CHILLI

(7) This chilli is not too hot and is great for bringing natural colour to a dish. It is used both whole, dried and ground, as well as in tempering (see page 21).

MUSTARD SEEDS

(8) Popular in western and southern Indian food, these are often tempered with oil, where they are brought to life, fizzing and popping in the pan, but take care – they can be quite lively. They can also be made into pastes.

STAR ANISE

(9) An important spice in my garam masala blend, star anise has a very sweet flavour, like liquorice. I use it in desserts, as well as in biryanis.

TURMERIC

(10) I use turmeric a lot, as I like its flavour – it looks like ginger and tastes and smells similar to raw mango. It brings colour to many dishes and drinks, used either in root form or ground.

(6)

(10)

(7)

(2)

(8)

(3)

GARAM MASALA

This is the most important spice blend for curries, and I make it regularly at home and in the restaurant. It is a key part of the recipes in this book, so it is worth keeping these spices in good quantities at home so you can mix it as needed. This is based on my mother's blend, which contains 16 different spices.

Makes 450g (1lb)

1 nutmeg
5 cinnamon sticks
3 tablespoons cloves
3 tablespoons sahi jeera (black cumin seeds)
5 tablespoons cumin seeds
10 whole black cardamoms
1 tablespoon whole green cardamoms
3 tablespoons kalpasi (black stone flower)
2 tablespoons fennel seeds
4–5 blades of mace
3 tablespoons whole black peppercorns
10 star anise
8 bay leaves
3 tablespoons coriander seeds
1 tablespoon fenugreek seeds
8–10 whole dried Kashmiri red chillies

Heat a pan and roast the spices on a low to medium heat until they begin to smell good, making sure they don't burn. Transfer them to a wide plate and leave to cool thoroughly, then blend to a fine powder in a spice blender. Sift and blend any coarse pieces again. Repeat if necessary. Store in an airtight glass jar.

GHATI MASALA

I was told about this blend during a conversation with a good friend who is a Mumbai Maharashtrian. It is common in Maharashtrian dishes, and is named after the ghats, or mountain passes, where the people live. It's used to make vada pao, a popular street food consisting of a bun with a potato patty, but I have used ghati masala with all kinds of vegetables, and serve it with tamarind and mint chutneys.

Makes 150g (5oz)

1 teaspoon rapeseed oil
8 garlic cloves
60g (2oz) grated dried coconut
1 tablespoon sesame seeds
1 tablespoon roasted peanuts
2 teaspoons red chilli powder
1 teaspoon ground coriander
½ teaspoon tamarind paste
salt

Heat the oil in a frying pan and roast the garlic cloves over a low heat for 1 minute. Turn off the heat and transfer the garlic to a plate.

Dry roast the coconut and sesame seeds over a low heat until the seeds start to pop (about 30 seconds), then transfer to the same plate.

Let the roasted garlic, coconut and sesame seeds cool for 5 minutes, then put them into a spice grinder or food processor with the remaining ingredients and grind them to a medium coarse powder. Taste for salt and add more if required.

Transfer to an airtight container. You can keep this for up to 15 days in the fridge.

CHETTINAD SPICE MIX

Chettinad in southern India is known for its vegetarian food.

Makes 350g (12¼oz)

10 tablespoons poppy seeds
8–10 fresh or dried curry leaves
5 tablespoons desiccated coconut
4 tablespoons fennel seeds
4–5 small cinnamon sticks
10 whole green cardamoms
10 cloves
4 star anise
4–5 red chillies
1 tablespoon kalpasi (black stone flower)
8 tablespoons coriander seeds

Heat a pan and dry roast the poppy seeds and curry leaves on a very low heat for about 10–12 minutes. Add the rest of the ingredients and continue roasting for another 8–10 minutes.

Remove from the heat and transfer to a tray or plate to cool down. Pour into a spice blender and grind to a fine powder.

Keep in an airtight container.

GODA MASALA

I use this spice mix from Maharashtra for my misal pao (see page 35), a beansprout curry that comes from that region. The rapeseed oil will naturally give this mix a wet texture, but if you prefer a powdered form, leave out the oil – it will keep for up to 1 month. It's also known as kala masala.

Makes 600g (1lb 5oz)

100ml (3½fl oz) rapeseed oil
3 tablespoons red chillies
3 tablespoons cumin seeds
3 tablespoons whole peppercorns
2 cinnamon sticks
3 tablespoons coriander seeds
3 tablespoons sahi jeera (black cumin seeds)
1½ tablespoons bay leaves
1½ tablespoons star anise
1½ tablespoons kalpasi (black stone flower)
3 whole nutmegs
3 tablespoons cloves
3 tablespoons mace
1½ tablespoons green cardamoms
3 tablespoons whole black cardamoms
1½ tablespoons Szechuan pepper

Heat the oil in a pan and shallow-fry all the spices on a medium heat, stirring regularly.

Once the flavours are released and the spices are starting to become lightly browned, remove from the heat. Drain in a fine sieve, discarding the oil, leave the spices to cool, then blitz in a spice blender – it will be a slightly wet mixture. Store in an airtight jar.

If you don't want to shallow-fry the spices, mix them together and dry roast them on a low heat instead.

GINGER/GARLIC PASTE

This paste plays a very important role in Indian cuisine – it's used in curries and makes a great marinade for meat, vegetables and seafood.

Makes 400g (14oz)

250g (9oz) garlic cloves
250g (9oz) fresh ginger root
1 teaspoon salt (optional)
3 tablespoons rapeseed oil

Peel the garlic. Wash the ginger roots, then peel and roughly chop them.

Put the chopped ginger and peeled garlic into a bowl and pour over enough water to cover. Leave them to soak for at least 1 hour, then drain off the water.

Put the soaked ginger and garlic into a blender and add the salt (if using) and the oil. (The salt and oil act as a preservative.)

Blend to a smooth paste, then transfer to a glass jar, close the lid tightly, and refrigerate.

CHILLI/GARLIC PASTE

This paste offers a big punch of flavour. It has a very limited shelf life, so I prefer to make it and consume it on the same day. Luckily, it is really easy to make.

Makes 50g (1¾oz)

2–3 green chillies
6–8 garlic cloves
1 tablespoon rapeseed oil

Wash the chillies, then remove the stem and seeds and roughly chop them. Peel the garlic.

Put the chopped chillies and peeled garlic into a blender and add the oil.

Blend to a smooth paste, then transfer to a glass jar, close the lid tightly, and refrigerate.

CASHEW NUT PASTE

Cashew nut paste is produced by blending cashews until they form a smooth paste. It's smooth and creamy and ideal for creating non-dairy milks, creams, smoothies, ice creams and sauces. It's also great for thickening sauces and curries.

Makes 300g (10½oz)

250g (9oz) cashew nuts
150ml (5fl oz) water

Soak the cashews in a bowl of cold water for 1 hour, then drain off the water and wash the cashews under running water.

Transfer the cashews to a food processor and blitz to a fine powder. Then slowly add the water to the granulated cashews and blend to a fine paste. If the mixture is grainy in texture, add more water and keep blending until you get the desired consistency – the paste should be smooth and creamy.

Store in an airtight container.

SPICED SALT

You can use this spiced salt with bread and butter to accentuate their flavours.

Makes 120g (4oz)

60g (2oz) cumin seeds
40g (1½oz) coriander seeds
1 teaspoon fenugreek seeds
2 whole dried red chillies
2 tablespoons black salt

Heat a pan and dry roast all the ingredients, except the black salt, on a very low heat.

Once the aromas are released, remove from the heat and transfer the spices to a tray or plate to cool down. Pour into a spice blender with the black salt and grind to a fine powder.

Keep in an airtight container.

SWEET YOGHURT

Sweet yogurt (meetha dahi) is very popular in northern India. It is very simple –just add sugar or honey, mix well and eat with a paratha or as a dip or side.

Makes 150g (5oz)

100g (3½oz) Greek yoghurt
50g (1¾oz) honey or sugar

Mix the yoghurt with the honey or sugar and chill in the fridge.

ONION PASTE

This delicious aromatic paste is made from slow-cooked onions, and is an essential ingredient in the Indian kitchen. It can be made by blending the onions alone, without other ingredients, or as here by including ginger/garlic paste.

Makes 275g (9½oz)

4 tablespoons rapeseed oil
250g (9oz) onions, sliced or chopped
2 tablespoons Ginger/Garlic Paste
   (see page 18)
1 teaspoon salt

Heat the oil in a non-stick pan on a medium-high heat. Add the onions and cook until they turn golden brown.

Add the Ginger/Garlic Paste and salt, and cook, stirring frequently, until the aroma of ginger and garlic disappears. Keep checking that the mixture doesn't catch on the bottom of the pan, which can happen very quickly.

Leave the onion mixture to cool down a little, then transfer it to a food processor while it's still warm and blitz to a fine paste. Leave to cool completely, then store in an airtight container in the fridge for up to 2–3 weeks.

FRIED ONIONS

Fried onions are an essential ingredient in the Indian kitchen, especially in biryanis and kebab dishes, and as a garnish. Blended with water and yoghurt, they make a base for vegetable, meat and fish curries, providing richness and body.

Makes 175g (6oz)

500ml (1 pint) rapeseed oil
250g (9oz) onions, finely sliced

Heat the oil to 170°C/340°F in a pan. Deep-fry the onions, moving them around until they turn golden brown, then remove with a slotted spoon and drain on a plate lined with kitchen paper. Leave to cool.

Once cool, store in an airtight container in a cool, dry place for up to 2–3 days.

TEMPERING (TADKA)

Also known as chhaunk in Hindi, this is the technique of frying spices quickly in oil or ghee. As they fry, their essential oils are released, and the aromatic oil and seeds are then poured over the dish. My mother used to make tadka in earthenware pots, because traditionally earthenware is believed not only to add flavour but also to preserve the nutritional qualities of the spices.

Nashta

BREAKFAST AND SNACKS

AKURI MASALA

Akuri is basically scrambled egg with onions and spices, and
a healthy and quick breakfast dish. Be careful not to overcook
the egg. There is a very similar dish called egg bhurjee, which
is also very popular in India.

6 eggs
2 tablespoons butter
4 garlic cloves, chopped
1 tablespoon chopped ginger
2 green chillies, deseeded and
    finely chopped
4 tablespoons finely chopped onion
½ teaspoon red chilli powder
¼ teaspoon ground turmeric
½ teaspoon garam masala
2 tablespoons deseeded and finely
    chopped tomato
2 tablespoons chopped coriander leaves
salt

Break the eggs into a bowl and add salt
to taste. Whisk the eggs thoroughly until
frothy, taking plenty of time over this.

Place a pan on a medium heat, then add the
butter and let it melt. Add the garlic, ginger,
green chillies and onions and sauté until the
onions are golden brown. Add the ground
spices and cook for another 2–3 minutes.

Add the tomatoes and cook until they turn
soft and release their juices.

Now add the egg mixture and allow it cook
for a minute, then gently scrape the sides
of the pan, slightly scrambling the eggs.
Stir it all up and once again allow it to cook
for a minute. Continue to gently scrape and
scramble until the eggs are cooked, but not
overcooked. They should be soft, slightly
runny and creamy, and not shredded into
separate bits.

Sprinkle over the chopped coriander,
mix well and turn off the heat.

Serve the akuri masala hot, with sliced
bread or toast and cups of tea or coffee.

ALOO PARATHA

Aloo paratha is one of the most popular breakfast dishes throughout western, central and northern regions of India.

2 medium potatoes, boiled and grated
2 tablespoons finely chopped
    coriander leaves
1 green chilli, finely chopped
¼ teaspoon toasted ground cumin
¼ teaspoon Garam Masala (see page 16)
¼ teaspoon dried mango powder (amchur)
¼ teaspoon red chilli powder
2 tablespoons rapeseed oil, for cooking
salt

FOR THE DOUGH
250g (9oz) wholemeal flour
1 teaspoon rapeseed oil
¼ teaspoon salt

First, make the dough. Mix together the wholemeal flour, oil and salt in a bowl. Mix in the water a little at a time, kneading as you go, until it forms a smooth, soft dough. You may not need to add all of the water. Cover and leave to rest for 15–20 minutes, then divide the dough into 4–6 equal parts.

To make the filling, put the grated potatoes into a bowl with the coriander, green chilli, toasted cumin, garam masala, dried mango powder, red chilli powder and some salt. Mix until everything is well combined.

To make the paratha, take a dough ball and roll it into a circle, using a rolling pin. Place 2–3 tablespoons of stuffing in the centre – don't overfill it, or it will be difficult to roll.

Bring all the edges together and pinch to seal, then flatten the ball using your hands.

Now roll the dough ball to a circle 18–20cm (7–8in) diameter. The trick here is to apply equal pressure while rolling. If you do that, your paratha will become round automatically.

Transfer the rolled paratha on to a hot griddle or tawa.

Cook on both sides for 1–2 minutes, then oil the side that's facing up and flip it over again. Now again oil the side that's facing up, so that both sides have been oiled. Press with a spatula and cook the paratha until both sides have golden brown spots on them.

Repeat with the rest of the dough balls.

Serve aloo paratha hot, with butter, pickles and a cup of chai!

CHOLE BHATURE

Chole bhature is one of my favourites among the delicious and flavourful dishes of Punjabi cuisine. Very well known and popular across India, this all-time favourite can be served at breakfast, lunch or dinner time. It's a spicy tangy chickpea curry, served with deep-fried fermented bread called bhature.

250g (9oz) chickpeas, soaked overnight (or you can use tinned chickpeas)
2 tea bags, or 2 tablespoons tea tied in a piece of muslin
4–5 whole black cardamoms
50ml (1¾fl oz) rapeseed oil
a pinch of asafoetida
150g (5oz) onions, chopped
1 tablespoon Ginger/Garlic Paste (see page 18)
2 teaspoons pomegranate powder
2 tablespoons ground coriander
½ teaspoon ground ginger
½ teaspoon ground turmeric
¼ teaspoon black salt
1 teaspoon ground cumin
1 tablespoon garam masala
70g (2½oz) tomato purée
2 tablespoons ginger julienne
4–5 green chillies, sliced
2 tablespoons chopped coriander leaves
2–3 lemon wedges, to serve
1 pickle dish, to serve
salt

FOR THE BHATURE

180g (6½oz) plain flour
60g (2oz) fine semolina
2–3 tablespoons vegetable oil
1 tablespoon sugar
1 teaspoon baking powder
70g (2½oz) natural yoghurt
oil, for deep-frying
a pinch of salt

Drain the soaked chickpeas, then cook them with the tea bags, black cardamoms and a little salt in a deep pan with plenty of water for at least 1–2 hours. If using tinned chickpeas, simmer them in a pan along with the tea bags, black cardamoms and a little salt for about 15–20 minutes until they become soft and turn brown in colour. Alternatively, you can use a pressure cooker.

Drain the chickpeas and set aside, discarding the spices and tea bags.

Heat 2 tablespoons of the oil in a pan, add the asafoetida and onions and sauté until the onions are golden brown. Add the Ginger/Garlic Paste and cook for couple of minutes until the raw aroma disappears.

Add the pomegranate powder, ground coriander, ground ginger, turmeric, black salt, cumin and garam masala, and cook for 2 minutes.

Add the tomato purée, mix well to combine, then add half the ginger julienne and the green chillies. Mix well again and cook for 5–6 minutes. Add the chickpeas and mix well, adding water if needed.

Cook, covered, over a low heat for 7–8 minutes, then check the seasoning, turn off the heat and set aside.

To make the dough, combine the flour, semolina, oil, salt, sugar and baking powder in a bowl. Add the yoghurt and mix well. Knead to a firm dough, then rub it with a little oil and cover with a muslin cloth.

Set aside to rise for 30–45 minutes.

Divide the dough into 6–8 equal portions.

Using a rolling pin, roll out each portion into an oval shape. Heat the remaining oil in a pan to 170°C/340°F. When it's hot, carefully slide the bhature into the pan and deep-fry for 3–4 minutes or until they puff up and both sides are slightly golden brown. (Pressing the centre lightly with a large spoon will help them to puff up while frying.)

Garnish the chickpeas with coriander and the rest of the ginger julienne. Serve with the hot bhature, alongside the pickle and some lemon wedges.

NOTE

Bhature is a fermented fried bread, made with yoghurt rather than yeast. It is slightly chewy in texture and mildly tangy in flavour.

PESARATTU

Pesarattu is a thin savoury breakfast pancake that is similar to a dosa – but with pesarattu, there's no fermentation, so it's much quicker and easier to make.

200g (7oz) whole mung beans
    (green gram)
2 tablespoons uncooked rice
2 green chillies
1 teaspoon cumin seeds
1 tablespoon chopped ginger
¼ teaspoon salt
2 tablespoons oil or ghee
Coconut Chutney (see page 168) or
    Tomato Chutney (see page 172), to serve

Put the mung beans and rice in a large bowl and rinse them well with cold water. Drain, then soak them in fresh water for about 4–6 hours. Drain the water and rinse the mung beans and rice well.

Put the mung beans, rice, green chillies, cumin seeds, ginger and salt in a food processor blender with just enough water to make a thick batter. Blend the ingredients to a slightly coarse or smooth batter to suit your liking – I usually blend to a semolina texture.

Pesarattu batter must be of pouring consistency yet thick and spreadable. If necessary, add more water. Do not make the batter runny, as the pesarattu will not become crispy.

Using a spatula, spread a little oil or ghee on a griddle or flat pan. Place over a medium–high heat.

Using a ladle, drop a spoonful of batter on to the hot pan and flatten quickly with the base of the ladle, until the surface is smooth. Cook for 2 minutes, then carefully flip and cook the other side, until crisp and brown.

Serve the pesarattu hot, with Coconut or Tomato Chutney.

OPTIONAL TOPPING

Heat 1 tablespoon ghee or oil in a pan. Add cumin seeds, onions and green chillies and sauté on a medium–high heat until transparent yet still crunchy, not soft. This will bring out the sweet flavour from the onions. Cool completely before serving.

IDLI SAMBHAR

Idli, a delicious southern Indian steamed rice cake that is slightly
fermented, is often served with sambhar (slow-cooked lentils with
vegetables and spices) and Coconut Chutney (see page 168).

FOR THE IDLI

200g (7oz) urad dal (split black gram),
    whole, without skin
1 teaspoon fenugreek seeds
800g (1lb 12oz) parboiled rice or idli rice
2 teaspoons salt

FOR THE SAMBHAR

250g (9oz) toor dal (yellow split peas)
½ teaspoon mustard seeds
a sprig of curry leaves
100g (3½oz) chopped onions,
    finely chopped
50g (1¾oz) desiccated coconut
½ teaspoon ground turmeric
½ teaspoon red chilli powder
1 tablespoon ground coriander
200g (7oz) pumpkin, diced
100g (3½oz) aubergines, diced
100g (3½oz) carrots, diced
100g (3½oz) bottlegourd, diced
1 green chilli, slit up one side
2 tomatoes, diced
50g (1¾oz) sambhar powder
50g (1¾oz) tamarind paste (see page 35)
a handful of coriander leaves
salt

FOR THE TADKA

2 teaspoons ghee or oil
½ teaspoon mustard seeds
½ teaspoon cumin seeds
½ teaspoon fenugreek seeds
1 sprig of curry leaves
½ teaspoon Kashmiri chilli powder
2 dried red chillies, broken into pieces
a pinch of asafoetida

To make the idli, rinse the urad dal under running water, then soak it in plenty of cold water with the fenugreek seeds for around 5–6 hours. At the same time, rinse the rice under running water until the water turns clear, then soak it in plenty of cold water for around 5–6 hours, the same time as the dal.

Drain the dal, then transfer it to a food processor or blender and add enough cold water to blend into a smooth thick paste. Put it into a bowl. Drain the rice and put it into the same food processor or blender, along with enough cold water to blend into a smooth paste. The amount of water you need will depend on the type of rice/dal you use. So, start with a lesser amount of water and add more as needed. Transfer the ground rice to the bowl of dal and add the salt.

Mix the batter for 1–2 minutes, using your hands – mixing by hand helps the fermentation process. The batter should be free-flowing, but it shouldn't be runny. Cover the bowl with a lid and place in a warm place overnight. After 8–10 hours it will be well fermented and should be frothy and bubbly. Set aside while you make the sambhar.

Wash the toor dal several times, then cook it in plenty of water in a deep pan on a medium heat for 15–20 minutes. Alternatively, you can use a pressure cooker. While the dal cooks, heat the oil in a heavy-based pan and add the mustard seeds. Once they start to pop, add the curry leaves and onion. Stir well and cook until brown. Add the desiccated coconut and ground spices and cook for another 2–3 minutes.

Add the diced vegetables and chilli and cook over a low heat until the vegetables are half cooked, then add the tomatoes. When the vegetables are completely cooked, add the sambhar powder and a little salt. Cook for 3–5 minutes.

Add the tamarind paste, filtered if you desire, then add the toor dal and 300ml (10fl oz) water and mix well to blend. Bring to the boil. Check if there is enough salt and sourness. If needed, add more salt and tamarind. Stir in the coriander leaves.

Meanwhile, make the tadka. Heat the oil or ghee in another pan. Add the mustard, cumin and fenugreek seeds and when they begin to sizzle, add the curry leaves, Kashmiri chilli powder and red chilli. When the leaves turn crisp, take off the heat and add the asafoetida. Pour this seasoning over the sambhar and stir well. Simmer for 2–3 minutes and the sambhar will become more flavourful.

To make the idli: grease some idli mould plates or shallow pudding bowls and fill them with the batter. Steam in a steamer for 10–12 minutes on a high heat. Cool for a minute or two, then take the idli out of the moulds. Serve with the sambhar and some Coconut Chutney.

MISAL PAO

Originating from Maharashtra, this beansprout curry uses a homemade Goda Masala (see page 17), a Maharashtrian spice blend. Traditionally, the dish is finished with onions, lemon and coriander, and is served with toasted and buttered buns.

200g (7oz) mixed beansprouts
½ teaspoon ground turmeric
3 tablespoons rapeseed oil
1 teaspoon mustard seeds
1 teaspoon cumin seeds
1 large or 2 medium onions, finely chopped
10–12 fresh curry leaves
1½ tablespoons Ginger/Garlic Paste
   (see page 18)
1–2 green chillies, finely chopped
1 teaspoon ground coriander
½ teaspoon red chilli powder
1–1½ tablespoons Goda Masala
   (see page 17)
1½ teaspoons tamarind paste (see below)
1 tablespoon chopped coriander leaves
2 tablespoons chopped onion, to garnish
lemon wedges and lemon zest, to serve
salt

Thoroughly rinse the beansprouts under cold running water, drain, then place in a pan of simmering water with ¼ teaspoon turmeric and a pinch of salt. Cook, covered, for about 10–12 minutes. Heat the oil in another pan, then add the mustard seeds. When they begin to pop, add the cumin seeds and sauté for a few seconds until they become golden.

Add the onions and sauté until they become translucent. Add the curry leaves, Ginger/Garlic Paste and green chillies and sauté, stirring, until the raw aroma of the ginger/garlic disappears.

Add the remaining turmeric, the ground coriander, red chilli powder and Goda Masala. Stir in the tamarind. If using your own tamarind paste, sauté until the raw aroma of the tamarind disappears.

Drain the cooked beansprouts, then stir into the pan with the onion mixture, adding 170–240ml (5¾–8fl oz) of water, if needed. The mixture should have a semi-thick consistency. Season with salt and simmer for 8–10 minutes on a low heat, stirring occasionally until thickened.

Just before serving, garnish with the coriander leaves, chopped onion, a lemon wedge and some grated lemon zest.

TO MAKE TAMARIND PASTE

Soak 50g (1¾oz) tamarind in 80–120ml (2¾–4fl oz) warm water for 25–30 minutes. Drain, squeezing out as much excess water as you can so that you are just left with the pulp.

PUNJABI SAMOSA

Samosas are one of my all-time favourite snacks. We used to eat these along with other street-food delicacies for breakfast every Sunday. A samosa is a savoury fried Indian snack that has a crispy outer crust flavoured with carom seeds and a spicy potato and green pea filling.

FOR THE DOUGH

½ teaspoon ajwain (carom seeds)
250g (9oz) plain flour or refined flour
60ml (2fl oz) vegetable oil, plus extra
    for kneading
a pinch of salt

FOR THE FILLING

400g (14oz) potatoes
1 tablespoon vegetable oil or ghee
½ teaspoon cumin seeds
1 tablespoon very finely chopped ginger
120g (4oz) frozen green peas
½ teaspoon red chilli powder
1 teaspoon Garam Masala (see page 16)
½ teaspoon ground cumin
½ teaspoon salt
½ teaspoon amchur (dried mango powder)
4 tablespoons finely chopped
    coriander leaves
8 cashews, chopped (optional)
1–2 green chillies, chopped (optional)
a pinch of asafoetida (optional)
oil, for deep-frying

First, make the filling. Boil the potatoes just until cooked – don't let them get mushy. Once they're cool, peel them, mash them with a fork and set aside.

To make the dough, mix the ajwain, flour, vegetable oil and salt in a mixing bowl. Rub the flour for 2–3 minutes between the palms of your hands, to incorporate the oil or ghee well. Take a handful of the flour and press it with your fingers. It must hold shape and not crumble. Add water little by little, about 50ml (1¾fl oz), mixing to form a dough. It has to be stiff and firm, not a soft dough. Cover and set aside for 25–30 minutes.

To make the filling, heat the oil or ghee in a pan and add the cumin seeds. When they begin crackling, add the ginger and cook until the raw aroma disappears. Stir in the peas and sauté for 2 minutes. Add the red chilli powder, garam masala and ground cumin and sauté for 30 seconds. Add the potatoes and sprinkle with the salt and dried mango powder. Stir and sauté for 2–3 minutes, then add the chopped coriander, taste, add more salt if needed, and set aside to cool.

Knead the dough to smooth it out a bit. Divide it into 5 portions and roll each one into a ball. Work on one ball at a time, covering the rest of the dough with a tea towel. Grease your work surface, then flatten one of the balls of dough and drizzle with oil.

Start to roll the dough out into an oval shape. It should be neither too thick nor too thin. Cut the oval in half diagonally and work with one half of the dough at a time. If the edges are too thick, gently roll the dough to thin them down.

Smear water over the straight edge, then join the edges to make a cone. Press gently to seal the cone from inside as well.

Fill the cone with the potato masala and press down. Smear the edges of the cone with water, then bring the edges together and make a pleat on one side. Fold back the pleat and seal it. Make sure the samosa has been sealed well. Heat the oil in a deep pan or kadai (see page 206) until medium hot, about 160°C/320°F.

Gently add as many samosas as you can to the oil and fry them on a low heat, undisturbed for a few minutes. When the crust firms up, flip them and continue to fry on a medium heat until crunchy and golden, then remove them to a colander.

While the first batch of samosas are frying, make the rest of them, letting the temperature of the oil reduce slightly before you fry the next batch.

Serve the samosas with Green Mint Chutney (see page 172) or Tomato Chutney (see page 172).

TO BAKE IN THE OVEN

Instead of deep-frying the samosas, preheat to 180°C/350°F/gas mark 4. Brush the samosa generously with oil and place on a prepared baking tray. Bake for 35–40 minutes.

VERMICELLI UPMA

This is also known as semiya upma – in India people usually make a sweet version with milk and dried fruits and traditionally it's always made with semolina, which is very popular in southern India. Here I have used vermicelli – it works really well as a quick and tasty alternative. It is also a great light lunch. *Pictured overleaf.*

1 tablespoon ghee or rapeseed oil
250g (9oz) vermicelli
2 tablespoons rapeseed oil
1 teaspoon mustard seeds
1 teaspoon urad dal (split black gram)
1 sprig of curry leaves
a pinch of asafoetida
50g (1¾oz) onions, chopped
2 green chillies, chopped
1 tablespoon chopped ginger
50g (1¾oz) French beans, cut into
　small dice
50g (1¾oz) carrots, cut into small dice
½ teaspoon red chilli powder
¼ teaspoon ground turmeric
50g (1¾oz) frozen green peas
½ teaspoon Garam Masala (see page 16)
salt, to taste

Heat the ghee in a large frying pan over a low heat. Add the vermicelli and sauté, stirring continuously, for 3–4 minutes or until golden. Set aside.

Heat the rapeseed oil in the same pan on a medium-high heat. Add the mustard seeds, urad dal and curry leaves and cook until they begin to crackle. Stir in the asafoetida. Add the onions, green chillies, ginger and a pinch of salt and sauté, stirring occasionally, for 2–3 minutes, or until the onions turn soft and translucent.

Add the beans and carrots and sauté for 4–5 minutes, or until the vegetables are half cooked, then add the chilli powder and turmeric. Pour in 240ml (8fl oz) of water, increase the heat and bring to the boil. Add the vermicelli and peas, then lower the heat to medium. Simmer until the vermicelli is cooked and the water has been absorbed. Check the seasoning, stir in the Garam Masala, and serve hot with a cup of tea.

CHILLA

Besan chilla, a protein-rich, nutritious pancake made from gram flour, is a popular snack from northern India. It's usually served with Coriander and Mint Chutney (see page 173).

250g (9oz) besan (gram flour)
½ teaspoon ajwain (carom seeds)
⅛ teaspoon ground turmeric
1 teaspoon grated ginger
3 tablespoons finely chopped tomatoes
3 tablespoons finely chopped onion
a handful of coriander leaves, chopped
1 green chilli, finely chopped
2 teaspoons rapeseed oil or ghee
salt

Put the gram flour, ajwain, turmeric and a pinch of salt into a mixing bowl. Mix everything well. Add the ginger, tomatoes, onions, coriander leaves and chillies. Gradually add enough water to make a thick but pourable batter.

Put a pan on a high heat and grease it lightly with few drops of oil. Once it's hot, reduce the heat to medium.

Stir the batter well, then take a ladleful and pour it into the centre of the pan, quickly spreading it into a round pancake. Drizzle some oil around the sides and in the centre and cook for a couple of minutes, until the edges of the pancake start to come away from the pan. Flip the pancake over on to the other side and press down the edges with a spatula. Fry until the chilla is cooked completely and has golden spots on it. Make the rest of the chilla the same way.

Serve with chutney and tea.

NOTE

Gram flour or besan is made from ground chickpeas. It has a wonderfully distinct and nutty flavour. It is naturally gluten-free and is widely used throughout Indian cuisine.

SABUDANA KHICHDI

Sabudana khichdi is very popular in northern India and is often made during the fasting season. It's very quick and easy to make. This khichdi doesn't use a lot of spices, and that's because a lot of spices are prohibited during fasting. If you are not making it for fasting, you can add more flavours and vegetables. It's a good option if you're gluten-free and vegan (serve it without yoghurt).

180g (6½oz) sabudana (tapioca pearls)
1 tablespoon groundnut oil (or optional
    clarified butter if not vegan)
½ teaspoon coarse black pepper
200g (7oz) potatoes, cut into small dice
2 tablespoons raw peanuts
1–2 green chillies, chopped
½ teaspoon salt, or to taste (use soondha
    namak if making this for fasting)
1 tablespoon chopped coriander leaves
2 tomatoes, cut into small dice
chilled yoghurt (optional), to serve

Rinse the sabudana under running water until the water turns clear. This is important, to get rid of all the starch. Transfer to a large bowl, add enough water to cover, and soak for at least 30–45 minutes.

By now it should have soaked up all the water. But you still need to drain it, using a colander to get rid of any excess. To check if the sabudana is ready to cook, press a pearl between your thumb and index finger. It should smash easily.

Heat the oil in a pan on a medium heat. Once it's hot, add the black pepper and the potatoes and cook for 3–4 minutes, stirring often, until the potatoes are almost cooked. Add the peanuts and green chillies and cook for another 2–3 minutes.

Add the drained sabudana to the pan along with the salt, coriander and tomatoes. Mix well.

Cook for a few minutes, until most of the sabudana pearls become translucent, stirring once or twice. Do not cook it for a long time or it will become sticky. Remove from the heat and serve hot, with some chilled yoghurt, if using.

BREAD PAKORA

This is a common street food that is popular for breakfast and evening snacks. Triangular bread slices are dipped in a spicy gram flour batter and fried. They can be stuffed or plain, but here we are using a potato stuffing. Serve them with mint or tomato ketchup for a perfect evening snack in the dark, cold months. I like to serve them with a cup of masala tea.

FOR THE STUFFING

180g (6½oz) potatoes, boiled and grated
  or mashed
1 teaspoon finely chopped green chillies
1 tablespoon finely chopped
  coriander leaves
1 teaspoon finely chopped mint leaves
¼ teaspoon red chilli powder
½ teaspoon turmeric
¼ teaspoon Garam Masala (see page 16)
¼ teaspoon amchur (dried mango powder)
salt

FOR THE BATTER

200g (7oz) besan (gram flour)
1¼ teaspoons red chilli powder
¼ teaspoon ground turmeric
½ teaspoon Garam Masala (see page 16)
a pinch of asafoetida
1 or 2 pinches of bicarbonate of
  soda (optional)

FOR THE PAKORAS

6 slices of wholemeal or white bread
oil, for deep frying

Put the grated or mashed potato into a bowl with the chillies, coriander, mint, chilli powder, turmeric, mango powder and a little salt and mix well. Check the seasoning and adjust accordingly. Set aside.

To make the batter, put the gram flour, chilli powder, turmeric, Garam Masala, asafoetida, bicarbonate of soda, if using, and a pinch of salt into a bowl. Add about 125ml (4¼fl oz) water and mix very well. The batter should be neither very thick nor too thin. If it is too thick, add more water.

Slice the bread into triangles or rectangles. Take about 2–3 tablespoons of the mashed potato mixture and spread it on the bread evenly. Cover with another slice of bread. You now have a triangular bread sandwich. Press it lightly, then dip it into the batter, coating evenly. Be gentle and take care not to leave it a long time in the batter, as the bread tends to break.

Heat enough oil in a deep frying pan for deep-frying, to about 170°C/340°F. Slide the batter-coated bread sandwiches into the hot oil and fry until they are crisp and golden brown. Drain them on kitchen paper, to absorb excess oil.

Serve the bread pakora hot or warm, with ketchup or Green Mint Chutney (see page 172).

POHA MASALA

Poha is a dish from the Indian states of Maharashtra, Odisha and
Madhya Pradesh, and it's also very popular where I was born, in
Gwalior. It's a light dish for breakfast or to have in the evening
with tea. It's made from poha, flattened rice, tossed with
a potato onion masala. Serve hot, with a dash of
lime juice and some fresh chopped coriander.

250g (9oz) poha (pressed rice),
   medium thick
2 tablespoons rapeseed oil
1 teaspoon mustard seeds
5–6 curry leaves
50g (1¾oz) chopped onions, plus extra
   to garnish
2 green chillies, slit down one side
1 teaspoon chopped ginger
2 potatoes, peeled and cut into small dice
100g (3½oz) frozen green peas
½ teaspoon red chilli powder
½ teaspoon Garam Masala (see page 16)
¼ teaspoon ground turmeric
½ teaspoon ground coriander
2 tablespoons chopped coriander leaves
4 tablespoons aloo bhujia
50g (1¾oz) chopped onions, to garnish
   (optional)
½ a lime, plus lime wedges to serve
salt

Rinse the poha in cold water and drain.
Set aside for 10 minutes.

Heat the oil in a pan. Add the mustard
seeds and curry leaves, and once they start
to crackle, add the onions and cook until
translucent. Add the green chillies and the
ginger and cook for 4–5 minutes.

Add the potatoes and peas and cook for
12–15 minutes on a low heat. Once the
veggies are cooked, add the chilli powder,
Garam Masala, turmeric and ground
coriander and mix well.

Add the drained *poha* and mix well.
Season with a little salt, mix well and cook
for 2 minutes. Top with a dash of lime juice
and serve hot, garnished with chopped
onion and lime wedges.

POORI BHAJI

This is a popular breakfast dish in northern India – a light, fragrant curry of spicy, softly mashed potatoes served with crusty, deep-fried bread. The perfect warming snack. *Pictured overleaf.*

FOR THE POORI

250g (9oz) wholemeal flour or
    multigrain flour
50g (1¾oz) semolina
a pinch of salt
2 tablespoons rapeseed oil, plus extra
    for deep-frying

FOR THE BHAJI

2 tablespoons rapeseed oil
1 teaspoon mustard seeds
1 teaspoon cumin seeds
1 green chilli, deseeded and finely chopped
1 tomato, roughly chopped
1 teaspoon red chilli powder
¼ teaspoon ground turmeric
2 teaspoons ground coriander
6 potatoes, boiled, peeled and cubed
½ teaspoon Garam Masala (see page 16)
5–6 sprigs of coriander leaves,
    finely chopped
salt

First prepare the poori. Put the flour and semolina into a bowl. Add the salt, rapeseed oil and enough water (60–80ml/2–2¾fl oz) to bring everything together, and knead to a stiff dough. Cover with a cloth and set aside for 15–20 minutes.

Next, make the bhaji. Heat the oil in a non-stick pan. Add the mustard and cumin seeds and let the mustard seeds crackle.

Add the green chilli and tomato and sauté until the tomato breaks down and becomes mushy. Stir in the chilli powder, turmeric and ground coriander and sauté on a low heat for 6–8 minutes. Check the consistency – if it's too thick, add 3–4 tablespoons water. Cook for a further 1–2 minutes.

Add the potato cubes and mix lightly. Season with salt to taste and again mix lightly. Add 240ml (8fl oz) water and cook on a low heat for a further 4–5 minutes, giving it an occasional stir, until thickened.

Divide the dough into 8–10 small equal portions, then gently roll each piece between your palms and shape into balls. Roll them out into small discs similar to roti

Pour enough rapeseed oil into a deep pan (kadai) to come at least halfway up the sides, and heat to a temperature of 170°C/340°F.

Deep-fry the discs in the hot oil for about 2–3 minutes, until they puff up and turn light golden brown. Drain on kitchen paper.

Lightly mash the potato cubes. Add 60ml (2fl oz) water and heat until the mixture comes to the boil. Stir in the Garam Masala and coriander, reserving some for a garnish, and mix well.

Put the fried pooris into a serving bowl. Put the potato bhaji into another bowl, garnish with the rest of the coriander, and serve hot.

BEDAI BHAJI

Crisp fried masala breads are stuffed with lentils and served with a coriander, black pepper and potato curry. This is another delicious street-food breakfast dish from New Delhi in northern India.

FOR THE BEDAI (STUFFED POORI)

250g (9oz) wheat flour
2 tablespoons semolina (sooji)
1 tablespoon ghee or oil
60g (2oz) urad dal (split black lentils),
    soaked in cold water for
    30 minutes, then drained
1 tablespoon fennel seeds
½ tablespoon ground coriander
½ teaspoon Garam Masala (see page 16)
¼ teaspoon ground black pepper
a pinch of salt
oil, for deep-frying

FOR THE SUBZI (CURRY)

2 tablespoons oil
1–2 bay leaves
4–5 cloves
2.5cm (1in) piece of cinnamon stick
4–6 whole black peppercorns
1 teaspoon cumin seeds
a pinch of asafoetida
2 large potatoes, peeled, boiled and
    mashed coarsely by hand
½ teaspoon red chilli powder
1 tablespoon ground coriander
1 teaspoon Garam Masala (see page 16)
1 tablespoon amchur (dried mango powder)
50g (1¾oz) coriander leaves, blended
    to a paste, plus extra leaves to garnish
2–3 green chillies, chopped, to garnish
salt

First, make the bedai. Combine the flour and semolina and add the ghee. Mix well and knead to a firm dough, adding a little water if required. Set aside, covered with a damp cloth, for 15 minutes.

Grind the soaked urad dal and fennel seeds separately. Mix them together and add the ground coriander, Garam Masala, black pepper, and salt. Mix thoroughly and set aside.

To make the curry, heat the oil in a deep saucepan and when it's hot, add the bay leaves, cloves, cinnamon stick, black peppercorns and cumin seeds. Add the asafoetida and the potatoes. Stir-fry for a minute, then add 675ml (1 pint 7fl oz) water. Bring to the boil, then cook for 2–3 minutes. Add the red chilli powder, ground coriander, Garam Masala, dried mango powder and a little salt to taste.

Cook for 5–7 minutes, adding more water if the consistency is too thick. Turn off the heat, stir in the fresh coriander paste and mix well.

Heat the oil to 160°C/320°F for deep-frying, in a medium pan on a low-medium heat.

Knead the dough once again and divide it into 8–10 dumplings. Roll them into rounds and make small pits by pressing with your thumb. Stuff 1 teaspoon of the urad dal filling into each of the bedai and enclose it with the dough. Using a greased rolling pin, roll them to a thickness similar to a roti and slide them gently into the hot oil. Deep-fry

on both sides for 2–3 minutes, flipping
them over until golden brown, then drain
on a plate lined with kitchen paper to
remove excess oil.

Reheat the potato curry, transfer to
a serving bowl and garnish with fresh
coriander leaves and green chillies.
Serve with the hot bedai.

Chakhna

SMALL SHARING PLATES

ALOO PYAZ MIRCH BHAJIA

These crispy pakoras are best served with green chutney and
hot tea . . . and sometimes with a slice of bread as well. This
is one of the most popular snacks during monsoon season
and winter time in India.

150g (5oz) onions, finely chopped
150g (5oz) potatoes, peeled and chopped
2 tablespoons chopped ginger
4 garlic cloves, chopped
5–6 Padrón chilli peppers or mild
    green chillies, deseeded and halved
    lengthways
5 tablespoons besan (gram flour)
1 teaspoon ajwain (carom seeds)
¼ teaspoon ground turmeric
½ teaspoon red chilli powder
250ml (8½fl oz) rapeseed oil,
    for deep-frying
½ teaspoon chaat masala (optional)

Put the onions, potatoes, ginger, garlic and
green chillies into a medium mixing bowl
and add the gram flour, ajwain, turmeric
and red chilli powder. Mix well with your
hands, adding a little water to coat and
bind everything together. Heat the oil in
a deep pan to 170°C/340°F. Once it's hot,
start dropping in spoonfuls of the vegetable
mixture – you can use your fingertips or
a tablespoon.

Deep-fry the pakoras until golden all over,
then drain on kitchen paper. Sprinkle with
the chaat masala, to serve.

TAREKO ALOO
(CRISPY FRIED POTATOES)

I love this dish, which I learnt to make when I went to Nepal
for my regional cuisine qualification, quite a long time ago now.
Nepali cuisine is robust and flavourful, a blend of Indian
and Tibetan influences.

2 teaspoons mustard oil
1 dried red chilli
¼ teaspoon ajwain (carom seeds)
2 garlic cloves, chopped
1 onion, sliced
1 tomato, deseeded and chopped
¼ teaspoon ground turmeric
½ teaspoon ground cinnamon
½ teaspoon ground cumin
750g (1lb 10½oz) fried potato slices
    (see below)
2 teaspoons lemon juice
1 spring onion, chopped
salt and pepper

Heat the oil in a pan, then add the dried red chilli, ajwain and garlic. Add the onions and tomatoes and sauté for 2 minutes.

Stir in the ground spices. Add the fried potato slices and lemon juice and cook for another 2 minutes. Season with salt and pepper to taste and scatter over the spring onion, to garnish.

TO MAKE FRIED POTATOES

Peel the potatoes, parboil for 5 minutes and drain. Slice into wedges about 2.5cm (1in) thick and, in batches, deep-fry in oil for 8–10 minutes at 170°C/340°F until light brown and crispy.

VANGI BHAAT

Vangi bhaat is a southern Indian dish that originated in Karnataka.
The literal translation is fried brinjal rice, but at Kutir I make it in
a different way, using an authentic recipe and experimenting with
different textures of aubergine.

2 aubergines
3 tablespoons rapeseed oil, or as needed,
   plus extra for deep-frying
1 sprig of curry leaves or 1 bay leaf
½ teaspoon mustard seeds or
   3 green cardamoms
100g (3½oz) onions, finely chopped
2 garlic cloves, finely chopped
1 green chilli, finely chopped
1 tablespoon finely chopped ginger
75g (2½oz) tomatoes, finely chopped
a pinch of asafoetida
200g (7oz) cooked plain rice
1 tablespoon lemon juice
salt
Chutney, to serve

**FOR THE VANGI BHAAT POWDER
(OR BUY IT READY-MADE)**

2 tablespoons coriander seeds
1 tablespoon chana dal (split chickpeas)
½ tablespoon urad dal (split black gram)
2–3 red chillies
½ teaspoon fenugreek seeds
1 teaspoon cumin seeds
4 cloves
1 small cinnamon stick

FOR THE COATING

2 teaspoons plain flour
6 tablespoons panko breadcrumbs

NOTE

You can buy both fresh or dried
curry leaves. I recommend using
fresh, if available, but either way,
these leaves will add richness,
depth and fragrance to your food.
They are edible, so don't worry
about removing these from the
dish before eating.

First make the vangi bhaat powder (skip this stage if you are using a ready-made powder). Dry roast the coriander seeds in a frying pan until crunchy and aromatic, and transfer them to a plate. Next roast the chana dal and urad dal. Add the red chillies and cook until the dal turns golden and aromatic. Add to the plate. Lastly add the fenugreek seeds, cumin seeds, cloves and cinnamon to the pan and sauté until the fenugreek seeds become aromatic. Cool all the spices completely, then grind them finely in a spice grinder or blender. Set aside.

Wash the aubergines and pat them dry with a tea towel. Rub them all over with oil and roast them on an open flame. (You can also grill the aubergines or roast them in the oven, but then you won't get the smoky flavour.) Keep turning the aubergines every 2–3 minutes on the flame, so that they cook evenly, and roast until completely cooked and tender. Remove from the heat and set aside to cool. Once cool, peel away the skin and chop the cooked aubergine finely, or mash it.

Heat the oil in a kadai or frying pan. Add the curry leaves and mustard seeds, and once they start to crackle, add the onions and garlic. Sauté the onions until they are golden brown, then add the green chillies and

ginger, followed by the tomatoes, and mix well. Cook, stirring often, until the tomatoes are pulpy and soft and the oil starts separating from the rest of the mixture.

Add the asafoetida and mix well. Stir in the chopped aubergine and season with salt, to taste. Sauté for 4–5 minutes more, then add the cooked rice and cook for another couple of minutes.

Add the vangi bhaat powder and check the seasoning, making sure the mixture is not too moist. Once ready, set aside and leave to cool.

Once cool, divide the mixture into equal-sized dumplings.

Mix the flour with a little water to make a semi-thick batter. Mix well, avoiding lumps. Put the panko breadcrumbs on a plate. Once your batter is ready, coat all the dumplings evenly, then roll them in the panko breadcrumbs so they are coated all over. The panko will give a crunchy texture.

Heat the oil to 170°C/340°F in a deep pan, and deep-fry the dumplings for 6–8 minutes or until they are golden brown all over. Drain on kitchen paper and serve with chutney.

CHICKPEA AND SAMPHIRE SALAD

Chana sundal is a healthy, low-fat and low-oil protein-rich snack and is generally served during religious festivals such as Navratri and Janmashtami. It's a southern Indian delicacy with an amazing flavour of grated coconut, asafoetida, curry leaves and mustard seeds. I have added fresh samphire to make it healthier, more interesting and seasonal.

1 tablespoon coconut oil or rapeseed oil
2 teaspoons black or brown mustard seeds
6 fresh curry leaves
3 dried Kashmiri chillies, broken into pieces, seeds removed
¼ teaspoon asafoetida (optional)
200g (7oz) tinned chickpeas, drained and rinsed
50g (1¾oz) fresh samphire
50g (1¾oz) freshly grated coconut, to garnish
1–2 lime wedges, to serve
salt

Heat the oil in a large frying pan over a medium-high heat. Add the mustard seeds, swirling the pan occasionally, and fry until the seeds begin to crackle. Add the curry leaves, chillies and asafoetida and cook, stirring occasionally, for about 45 seconds or until the curry leaves have slightly darkened.

Add the chickpeas and cook, tossing often, for about 3 minutes, until just warmed through. Leave to cool, then add the fresh samphire and season with salt, to taste.

Garnish with fresh coconut and serve with lime wedges.

> **NOTE**
>
> Asafoetida is a combination of dried gum resins from plant roots, and is available at Indian food shops and some supermarkets.

CHANDNI CHOWK KI ALOO TIKKI

Chandni Chowk is very famous in Delhi for its street food and chaat (snack) preparations. Aloo tikki chaat is well-known in Mumbai and northern India, and can now be found all over the country, even in small eateries and roadside stalls. The crunchy tikkis, or patties, are made of potatoes and spices, and here I've turned them into a sharing plate or starter by cooking the peas separately and plating the tikki on top of the masala.

FOR THE GREEN PEA MASALA

100g (3½oz) dried green peas, soaked
   for a couple of hours or overnight
1 tablespoon rapeseed oil
1 teaspoon cumin seeds
1 onion, finely chopped
½ teaspoon Ginger/Garlic Paste
   (see page 18)
¼ teaspoon asafoetida
1½ teaspoons ground coriander
¼ teaspoon ground turmeric
1 teaspoon red chilli powder
1 teaspoon Garam Masala (see page 16)
100g (3½oz) tomatoes, chopped
salt

FOR THE ALOO TIKKI

4 potatoes, boiled, peeled, then grated
½ teaspoon amchur (dried mango powder)
½ teaspoon cumin seeds, toasted
1 green chilli, finely chopped
1 teaspoon chopped fresh ginger
1 tablespoon finely chopped coriander
   leaves (optional)
2 tablespoons potato flour
2 tablespoons cornflour
250ml (8½fl oz) rapeseed oil
salt

FOR THE ACCOMPANIMENTS

2 tablespoons Sweet Yoghurt (see page 20)
   or curd
Green Mint Chutney (see page 172)
Tamarind Chutney (see page 176)
2 tablespoons sev (optional)
1 tablespoon chopped coriander leaves
100g (3½oz) white radish, cut into
   julienne strips
50g (1¾oz) onion, pickled or fresh,
   finely sliced

First, make the green pea masala. Drain the dried peas, then put them into a large pan with plenty of water and cook for about 40 minutes, until they are tender. Drain and set aside.

Place a non-stick pan on a medium heat and add the oil. Once it's hot, add the cumin seeds. When they start to crackle, add the onion and sauté until it becomes golden brown.

Add the Ginger/Garlic Paste and sauté until the raw aroma disappears. Add the asafoetida, ground coriander, turmeric, red chilli powder and Garam Masala and sauté for a minute, then add the tomatoes. Cook on a low heat for 3–4 minutes, or until oil starts to appear at the edge of the pan. Add the dried peas and season with salt to taste. Add 240ml (8fl oz) water, cover with a lid and bring to the boil. Reduce the heat as low as possible and simmer for 7–8 minutes. The peas will thicken the mixture and absorb the aroma of the spices.

Next make the aloo tikki. Put the potatoes into a bowl. Add the dried mango powder, cumin seeds, green chilli, ginger, coriander (if using) and a little salt, mix well, then add the potato flour and cornflour. Mix together thoroughly, then divide into 10 equal portions and shape into patties.

Heat the oil to 170˚C/340˚F in a deep pan and deep-fry 3–4 patties at a time until all sides are golden brown and crisp, about 6–8 minutes.

Pour some of the pea masala into each serving bowl and add 2 aloo tikki. Drizzle over some Sweet Yoghurt, Green Mint Chutney and the Tamarind Chutney, sprinkle with the sev, if using, and the coriander and garnish with radish and sliced onion.

STUFFED SWEET PEPPERS

Bharwan mirch (stuffed pepper) dishes are very popular in northern India. These could be served as a starter or as a main course, with an onion and tomato based gravy.

12 small sweet peppers (available
    at the supermarket)
100g (3½oz) paneer
50ml (1¾fl oz) rapeseed oil
1 teaspoon cumin seeds
1 tablespoon chopped ginger
2–3 green chillies, deseeded and chopped
⅓ teaspoon ground turmeric
a pinch of asafoetida
100g (3½oz) potatoes, boiled and grated
½ teaspoon Garam Masala (see page 16)
½ teaspoon amchur (dried mango powder)
2 tablespoons chopped coriander leaves
salt
Green Mint Chutney (see page 172) or Raw
    Mango Chutney (see page 171), to serve

FOR THE MARINADE
2 tablespoons Greek yoghurt
½ tablespoon Ginger/Garlic Paste
    (see page 18)
½ a green chilli, chopped
½ teaspoon Kashmiri chilli powder
½ teaspoon dried fenugreek leaves
1 teaspoon lime juice
1 tablespoon rapeseed oil
1 sprig of coriander, chopped
½ teaspoon Garam Masala (see page 16)

First of all make a slit in each pepper and remove the seeds. Set the peppers aside.

Grate the paneer into a bowl. Heat the oil in a pan and add the cumin seeds. Once they start crackling, add the ginger and green chillies and stir well. Cook for 2–3 minutes, then add the turmeric, asafoetida, grated paneer and a little salt. Mix well and cook for another 4–5 minutes. Add the potatoes, Garam Masala and dried mango powder. Check the seasoning, then turn down the heat and add the chopped coriander. Mix well, then set aside and let the mixture cool.

Stuff the cooled paneer mixture into the peppers, pressing it in firmly. Set aside.

Mix all the marinade ingredients together in a small mixing bowl.

Spoon the marinade evenly over the stuffed peppers and transfer them to the fridge for at least 1–2 hours.

Preheat the oven to 180°C/350°F/gas mark 4.

Arrange the marinated peppers on a non-stick baking tray and cook in the oven for 10–15 minutes.

Once the peppers are charred on the outside, take them out of the oven and serve with chutney.

TAWA SALAD

Seasonal greens are marinated with kasundhi (Indian mustard paste) and spices, and tossed on a tawa (griddle) to make an amazing salad for your lunch or as an excellent side.

100g (3½oz) small golden or red
   beetroots, washed
8–10 asparagus spears, peeled
   and trimmed
2 carrots, cut into 5cm (2in) batons
6–8 French beans, halved
6–8 broccoli florets or tenderstem broccoli
1 tablespoon kasundhi (optional)
½ teaspoon coarse black peppercorns
1 tablespoon olive oil
25g (1oz) chopped onion
1 tablespoon chopped ginger
1 tablespoon chopped coriander leaves
salt

FOR THE DRESSING

50ml (1¾fl oz) olive oil
½ a bunch of coriander roots
¼ teaspoon ground black pepper
juice of 1 lime
¼ teaspoon sugar

Preheat the oven to 180°C/350°F/gas mark 4. Wrap the beetroots in tin foil and roast for about 10–12 minutes.

Bring a pan of water to the boil, add salt and blanch the asparagus, carrots, beans and broccoli. Drain, then drop into ice-cold water and set aside.

When the beetroots are ready, let them cool, then unwrap and cut them into 5cm (2in) batons, similar to the carrots.

Drain the asparagus, carrots, beans and broccoli and transfer them to a bowl with the beetroot. Add the kasundhi, if using, peppercorns, olive oil and a little salt. Mix well and let them marinate for 15–20 minutes.

Blitz together all the ingredients for the dressing in a blender.

Heat a non-stick pan and add a few drops of oil. Add the marinated vegetables in one layer and griddle them evenly. Put them into a bowl and add the onion, ginger, coriander and the dressing. Mix well and serve warm.

LOTUS ROOT CHILLI FRY

Lotus roots are the stems of the lotus plant and are very popular in Asian countries and Chinese cuisine. This recipe is another favourite and is hugely popular back home in India. Crispy fried lotus root is tossed in a flavourful spicy sauce made with soy, chilli, tomato ketchup and vinegar.

3 tablespoons cornflour
3 tablespoons plain flour
¼ teaspoon red chilli powder
a pinch of coarsely ground black pepper
a pinch of salt
350ml (12fl oz) oil
200g (7oz) lotus root, cut into rounds or diced and rinsed in cold water
1 tablespoon finely chopped garlic
2 spring onions, chopped (white and green parts separated)
1 onion, quartered, layers separated
1 green chilli, slit and deseeded
½ a green pepper, diced
¼ teaspoon crushed black peppercorns

FOR THE SAUCE

1 teaspoon cornflour
2 tablespoons red chilli sauce
1 tablespoon soy sauce
2 tablespoons tomato ketchup
1 teaspoon sugar
½ teaspoon vinegar (I use apple cider vinegar)
½ teaspoon red chilli powder (optional)

TIP

Fresh lotus root can be bought online or at specialist food shops. However, if you can't get hold of any fresh, you can use tinned lotus root instead.

Put the cornflour and plain flour into a mixing bowl. Add the red chilli powder, black pepper, salt and a little water. Mix together to make a batter.

Heat the oil in a deep pan to 170°C/340°F.

Gently coat the pieces of lotus root with the batter. Check if the oil is hot enough by dropping in a small spoonful of the batter. It must rise without browning. When this happens, the oil is at the correct temperature. Pick up each batter-coated piece of lotus root with a spoon and gently slide them into the hot oil. Stir and fry them on a medium heat on all sides until crispy, about 3–4 minutes. Drain on kitchen paper.

To make the sauce, put the cornflour into a bowl and mix with 125ml (4¼fl oz) water. Stir well and set aside. In another small bowl, mix together the chilli sauce, soy sauce, ketchup, sugar, vinegar and red chilli powder (if using). Set this aside.

Remove the excess oil from the pan, retaining 1 tablespoon. Add the garlic and fry until the raw aroma disappears. Add the spring onion whites, onions, green chilli and diced green pepper and sauté on a high heat for 2 minutes.

Stir the chilli/soy sauce mixture and add it to the pan.

Stir the prepared cornflour slurry and add it to the pan. Mix everything together well and cook on a medium heat until the sauce thickens. Check the taste. You can add more sauces or salt if you wish, to adjust to your own taste. If you want to thin down the sauce, just add enough hot water to get the desired consistency.

Turn off the heat and let the sauce cool down slightly. Then add the crushed black peppercorns and fried lotus root cubes to the sauce and mix. Scatter over the spring onion greens. Serve hot, as an appetizer.

BEETROOT CUTLETS

This is a delicious Kolkata-style dish of potatoes, beetroot and peanuts, made into spicy cutlets using a variety of spices.

½ teaspoon cumin seeds
½ teaspoon fennel seeds
6 cloves
3 green cardamoms
1cm (½in) piece of cinnamon stick
10 peppercorns
2–3 dried red chillies
1–2 bay leaves
1 teaspoon rapeseed oil, plus extra
    for deep-frying
2 teaspoons peanuts, plus extra to garnish
1 teaspoon grated ginger
2 green chillies, finely chopped
2 beetroots, finely grated
2 carrots, finely grated
2 small potatoes, boiled and mashed
a handful of coriander leaves,
    finely chopped
salt and sugar, to taste

FOR THE COATING

2 teaspoons plain flour
5–6 tablespoons panko breadcrumbs

Dry roast the cumin seeds, fennel seeds, cloves, green cardamoms, cinnamon, peppercorns, chillies and bay leaves on a slow heat. Once you start smelling the aromas of the spices, remove the pan from the heat. Transfer the spices to a plate and leave to cool, then grind in a spice grinder and set aside.

Heat 1 teaspoon oil in a kadai or frying pan and lightly fry the peanuts. Remove them from the pan and set aside. In the same oil, fry the ginger and green chillies until they start to give off a light aroma.

Add the grated beetroot and carrot and sauté well. Add the mashed potatoes, the ground roasted spice powder, coriander, and a little salt and sugar. Mix well and set aside until cool.

Once the mixture has cooled, shape it into 15–20 balls. Heat the oil to 170°C/340°F for deep-frying in a deep pan.

In a bowl, mix the flour with a little water to make a thin white batter. It shouldn't be too thick. Put the panko breadcrumbs on a plate. Roll each ball first in the batter, then in the breadcrumbs, and deep-fry them in the hot oil for 6–8 minutes or until golden brown.

Serve the beetroot cutlets piping hot, with some onion rings, ketchup or, like they do in Kolkata, with the shop-bought tangy mustard sauce called kasundhi.

APPLE AND ROOTS DHOKLA SALAD

Dhokla is pretty popular in Gujarati cuisine, and easy to make,
with just a handful of basic ingredients. Here I make it into
a salad, with a combination of root vegetables and apple. Dhokla
is all about assembling interesting flavours and getting the
right balance of ingredients.

150g (5oz) besan (gram flour), sifted
215g (7½oz) yoghurt, beaten
½ teaspoon salt
½ teaspoon ground turmeric
1 teaspoon Chilli/Garlic Paste
   (see page 18)
1 tablespoon lemon juice
1 teaspoon bicarbonate of soda
2 tablespoons vegetable oil
2 green apples
4–5 candy beetroot or mixed-colour
   heritage baby beetroot
1 teaspoon beetroot powder
1 teaspoon mustard seeds
6–8 curry leaves
2 tablespoons vinegar
1 tablespoon sugar
2 tablespoons chopped coriander leaves
50g (1¾oz) grated coconut
1 tablespoon Ghati Masala (see page 16)
salt

Put the gram flour into a bowl. Add the
yoghurt and about 225ml (7½fl oz) warm
water and mix, avoiding lumps. Add the salt
and mix again. Leave aside to ferment for
3–4 hours.

When the gram flour mixture has fermented,
stir in the turmeric and the Chilli/Garlic
Paste. Heat a steamer, and grease a thali.

Put the lemon juice, bicarbonate of soda
and 1 teaspoon of the oil into a small bowl
and mix. Add this to the fermented batter
and whisk briskly. Pour the batter into the
greased thali and place it in the steamer.

Cover with the lid and steam for 10 minutes.
When cooled a little, cut the dhokla into
squares and place in a serving bowl or on
a plate.

Meanwhile, peel the apples, cut into wedges,
and set aside in a bowl of water with lemon
juice added. Wash the beetroots and blanch
in boiling water, then drain and set aside
to cool.

Put the beetroot powder into a bowl and stir
in 225ml (7½fl oz) water. Add the soaked
apple and candy beetroot.

Heat the remaining oil in a small pan. Add
the mustard seeds and curry leaves. When
the seeds begin to crackle, add the vinegar,
sugar and 200ml (7fl oz) water, then remove
from the heat and pour over the dhoklas.

Arrange the soaked apple and beetroot on
a plate, along with the dhoklas. Scatter over
the chopped coriander leaves and grated
coconut, and sprinkle the Ghati Masala
on top.

SUN-DRIED TOMATO AND ASPARAGUS ROLLS

This is one of my favourite vegan dishes. I make these like Sri Lankan-style rolls, stuffed with spiced veg and coated with crumbs and spices.

2 tablespoons rapeseed oil, plus extra
   for deep-frying
2 tablespoons chopped onion
1 tablespoon chopped ginger
1 tablespoon chopped green chilli
1 tablespoon chopped curry leaves
2 garlic cloves, chopped
50g (1¾oz) frozen green peas
50g (1¾oz) French beans, blanched
   and cut into batons
100g (3½oz) asparagus, blanched and
   cut into batons
¼ teaspoon ground cinnamon
½ teaspoon coarsely ground black pepper
100g (3½oz) potatoes, boiled and grated
10 spring roll wrappers
50g (1¾oz) sun-dried tomatoes
150g (5oz) panko breadcrumbs

FOR THE BATTER
4 tablespoons wheat flour
salt

Heat the oil in a frying pan. Add the onion, ginger, green chilli, curry leaves and garlic and sauté until the onion turns light golden. Add the frozen peas, beans, asparagus, cinnamon, black pepper and a pinch of salt. Cook for 3–4 minutes, then add the grated potatoes and mix well. The mixture shouldn't be too runny, otherwise it will be difficult to handle while making the spring rolls. Check the seasoning and set aside to cool.

Lay a spring roll wrapper in front of you. Add 1 tablespoon of the vegetable mixture, put one piece of sun-dried tomato in the centre, and roll up tightly.

Put the flour into a bowl with a pinch of salt and enough water to make a runny batter. Put the panko crumbs into a dish alongside.

Once each roll is ready, dip it first into the batter and then roll it over the panko crumbs so it's coated evenly. Once done, put the rolls into the fridge for 10–15 minutes.

Heat the oil to 170°C/340°F and deep-fry the rolls for 6–8 minutes until crisp and golden brown. Serve hot, with your choice of chutney.

KIDNEY BEAN KEBAB

These kebabs are packed with flavour and melt in the mouth. I tried them for the first time when I visited Lucknow, in northern India, which is famous for biryani and kebabs. This rajma galouti kebab is a vegetarian version of the traditional galouti kebab, replacing meat with kidney beans.

200g (7oz) cooked rajma (kidney beans) or tinned kidney beans
2 tablespoons chopped mint leaves
1 tablespoon dried rose petals
50g (1¾oz) onions, sliced and fried
1 green chilli
1 tablespoon chopped ginger
3 garlic cloves, fried
50g (1¾oz) fried cashew nuts
100g (3½oz) potatoes, boiled and grated
1 teaspoon rose water
1 teaspoon Garam Masala (see page 16)
1 teaspoon chaat masala
2 tablespoons besan (gram flour)
100ml (3½fl oz) rapeseed oil, for frying
salt
Green Mint Chutney (see page 172), to serve

If you are cooking the kidney beans, soak them in cold water for at least 8 hours, then cook them in plenty of salted boiling water for 40–50 minutes on a low heat, until they are very soft. Alternatively, you can use a pressure cooker. Once the kidney beans are cooked completely, drain and set aside.

To make the kebabs, put the mint leaves, dried rose petals, fried onions, green chilli, ginger, garlic and cashew nuts in a food processor and blend to a coarse mixture. Add the drained kidney beans and blend again. Put the mixture into a large mixing bowl, add the rest of the ingredients, except the oil, and knead well.

Divide the mixture into 8–10 equal portions and shape each one into a circular disc.

Preheat a frying pan and grease it with oil. Add the kebabs a few at a time and drizzle a few drops of oil over them, then pan-fry them on both sides for about 6–8 minutes until lightly crisp.

Place on a serving platter and serve with the chutney.

MALABAR CAULIFLOWER

Malabar cauliflower is a spicy, deep-fried dish originating from Chennai, in southern India. I make it as a quick snack and slightly tweak the recipe using Malabar pepper, one of the best quality black peppercorns. If you can't find Malabar pepper, it is fine to use regular black pepper. **Pictured overleaf.**

200g (7oz) cauliflower, cut into
   small florets
2 sprigs of curry leaves, finely chopped
2 teaspoons mild red chilli powder
juice of 1 lime
2 tablespoons rice flour
3 tablespoons cornflour
2 green chillies, deseeded and
   finely chopped
½ teaspoon Garam Masala (see page 16)
1½ teaspoons Ginger/Garlic Paste
   (see page 18)
¼ teaspoon ground Malabar pepper,
   or other ground black pepper
250ml (8½fl oz) rapeseed oil, for
   deep-frying
1 tablespoon chopped coriander leaves
1 tablespoon grated fresh coconut
salt
Tomato Chutney (see page 172), to serve

Put the cauliflower florets into a bowl with the curry leaves, 1 teaspoon of the red chilli powder, the lime juice and a pinch of salt and set aside to marinate.

Make a batter using the rice flour, cornflour, green chillies, Garam Masala, Ginger/Garlic Paste, the remaining teaspoon of red chilli powder, black pepper and a pinch of salt. Add water as needed – the batter shouldn't be too runny or too thick, just enough to coat the cauliflower with a thin layer.

Heat the oil to 170°C/340°F in a large pan. Dip the marinated cauliflower into the batter and deep-fry on a medium heat until cooked and crispy, about 3–4 minutes. Set aside on kitchen paper to drain the excess oil. Serve hot, with chopped coriander and grated coconut sprinkled on top and a dollop of chutney.

DAL CHAWAL AUR ACHAR

Dal chawal is a staple food of India. Most people use yellow dal in this dish, but I have given it a twist. Rather than serving as a main course, these are panko-coated deep-fried dumplings to serve with classic accompaniments like raita, pickle and poppadums.

60g (2oz) basmati rice
100g (3½oz) toor dal (yellow split peas)
4 teaspoons rapeseed oil, plus extra for
    deep-frying
1 teaspoon cumin seeds
1 tablespoon chopped ginger
1 green chilli, chopped
50g (1¾oz) onions, chopped
1 tablespoon chopped garlic
1 teaspoon red chilli powder
1 teaspoon ground turmeric
50g (1¾oz) tomatoes, chopped
2 tablespoons chopped coriander leaves
100g (3½oz) cornflour
150g (5oz) panko breadcrumbs
salt

FOR THE TADKA DAHI

100g (3½oz) plain yoghurt
3 tablespoons rapeseed oil
¼ teaspoon mustard seeds
3 curry leaves, chopped
a pinch of ground turmeric
½ teaspoon chopped ginger
½ teaspoon chopped green chilli

Soak the rice in cold water for 20 minutes, then drain. Cook in a pan of boiling water until tender, drain and set aside. Soak the toor dal in cold water for 20 minutes, then cook with a little salt and turmeric for about 15 minutes on a medium heat, until soft. Once cooked, set aside.

Heat the oil in a pan, then add the cumin seeds, ginger and green chillies and sauté for a few minutes. Add the onion and garlic and cook until golden. Add the chilli powder, turmeric and salt to taste and cook for a minute or so, then add the chopped tomatoes and cook until they become soft. Add the cooked toor dal and the coriander. Stir in the cooked rice and turn off the heat. Once cool, check the seasoning and, if required, add more salt and ginger, further green chilli and more coriander.

Make sure the mixture is not too wet – you need to be able to shape it into dumplings. Let it cool, then divide it into equal-sized dumplings and put them into the fridge for 30–45 minutes.

Put the cornflour into a small bowl and add enough water to make a thin batter. Put the panko breadcrumbs on a plate. Dip the dumplings into the batter, then roll them evenly in the panko breadcrumbs. Heat the oil to 170°C/340°F and deep-fry the dumplings until they are crisp and golden. Drain on kitchen paper.

To prepare the tadka dahi, whisk the yoghurt in a bowl, add a little salt and set aside. Heat the oil in a small pan and add the mustard seeds and curry leaves. Once the seeds start to crackle, add a pinch of turmeric and the ginger and green chilli. Sauté for a minute, then gently stir in the yoghurt. Remove from the heat and serve the tadka dahi with the hot dumplings.

BHARWAN GUCHHI
(STUFFED MORELS)

Stuffed morels are a very good option for vegetarians. Morels are one of the most expensive exotic ingredients grown in Kashmir, and they are always in high demand because of their flavour and texture. I use Kashmiri morels at the restaurant, but use any type that you prefer.

6–8 medium dried morels
50ml (1¾fl oz) rapeseed oil
1 teaspoon cumin seeds
100g (3½oz) mixed wild mushrooms, roughly chopped
2–3 green chillies, seeded and chopped
1 tablespoon chopped ginger
1 tablespoon chopped garlic
a pinch of asafoetida
⅓ teaspoon ground turmeric
50g (1¾oz) potatoes, cooked and grated
½ teaspoon amchur (dried mango powder)
2 tablespoons chopped coriander leaves
½ teaspoon Garam Masala (see page 16)
salt

FOR THE MARINADE

2 tablespoons Greek yoghurt
½ tablespoon Ginger/Garlic Paste (see page 18)
½ a green chilli, chopped
1 teaspoon lime juice
1 tablespoon rapeseed oil
1 sprig of coriander, chopped
½ teaspoon Garam Masala (see page 16)

Soak the morels in water for an hour. Once they are soft, drain them, clean them carefully, pat dry and set aside.

Heat the oil in a pan and add the cumin seeds. Once they start to crack, add the chopped mixed mushrooms and green chillies and cook on a high heat until caramelised. Turn down the heat, add the ginger and garlic and cook for another 4–5 minutes until the raw smell goes away. Add the ground spices and cook for another 2 minutes. Add the grated potatoes and dried mango powder, mix well, then check the seasoning and set aside to cool.

Press the cooled mushroom mixture firmly into the morels.

Mix all the marinade ingredients together in a small bowl. Spread the marinade evenly over the stuffed morels and put them into the fridge for at least 1–2 hours.

Preheat the oven to 180°C/350°F/gas mark 4. Arrange the marinated morels on a non-stick baking tray and cook in the oven for 10–15 minutes.

Once the morels begin to look charred, remove from the oven and serve hot, with Green Mint Chutney (see page 172).

TOFU AND GREEN PEA TIKKI

Tofu, also known as bean curd, is a food prepared by coagulating soy milk and then pressing the resulting curds into solid white blocks of varying softness. You can buy versions that are silken, soft or firm. Tofu is a great substitute for paneer if you are vegan. This combination of tofu and green pea is wonderful.

2 tablespoons rapeseed oil
1 tablespoon cumin seeds
1 tablespoon finely chopped ginger
1 tablespoon finely chopped green chilli
a pinch of asafoetida
150g (5oz) green peas, cooked
    and crushed
½ tablespoon roasted ground cumin
1 teaspoon red chilli powder
300g (10½oz) tofu, grated or crumbled
1 tablespoon finely chopped
    coriander leaves
2 tablespoons cornflour
oil, for shallow-frying
salt

TO SERVE
Green Mint Chutney (see page 172)
ketchup
a few mint leaves
a few coriander leaves

Heat the oil in a non-stick kadai or pan. Add the cumin seeds, ginger and green chilli and sauté until they start to crackle.

Add the asafoetida and mix well. Add the peas and mix well, then add the roasted cumin, red chilli powder and salt to taste. Break down the peas with a spoon and cook for a minute. Add the tofu and the chopped coriander. Mix well, then transfer to a bowl and set aside.

Put the cornflour into a bowl and mix with enough water to make a batter – not too thick or too thin, just enough to coat the tikkis. Heat the oil for shallow-frying in a non-stick pan.

Shape the pea mixture into patties, dip them into the cornflour batter and fry until evenly golden on both sides, about 6–8 minutes. Drain on kitchen paper.

Place the tikkis on a serving plate. Top with chutney, ketchup, garnish with mint and coriander leaves and serve hot.

SEASONAL GREENS COUSCOUS SALAD

Couscous has a light fluffy texture and has become a very popular alternative to rice and pasta and is very easy to cook. Here it's served with seasonal greens and vegetables.

½ teaspoon salt
2 tablespoons extra virgin olive oil
140g (5oz) instant couscous

FOR THE SALAD

8 small broccoli florets
8 mangetout, sliced
60g (2oz) carrots, cut into small dice
1 teaspoon olive oil
2 garlic cloves, crushed
6 dried apricots, cut into small dice
1 tablespoon chopped coriander leaves

FOR THE LEMON DRESSING

1 teaspoon grated lemon zest
2 tablespoons lemon juice
2 tablespoons rice vinegar
¼ teaspoon salt
¼ teaspoon freshly ground black pepper
4 tablespoons olive oil

Put 180ml (6fl oz) water into a medium pan with the salt and olive oil and bring to the boil. Add the couscous and stir quickly, then turn off the heat and cover the pan.

Let it stand for about 5 minutes until the couscous is tender, then fluff with a fork and set aside to cool.

Bring a pan of salted water to the boil, and blanch the broccoli, mangetout and carrots. Drain and set aside.

To make the dressing, whisk together the lemon zest, lemon juice, rice vinegar, salt and pepper in a small bowl. Slowly drizzle in the olive oil, whisking until a thick dressing forms.

Heat the olive oil in a small pan and sauté the garlic, then add the blanched vegetables and the diced apricots and mix well. Remove from the heat, add the dressing and the couscous and stir to combine. Check the seasoning and serve warm, sprinkled with the coriander.

NOTE

Couscous is made from tiny granules of dried durum wheat, and contains carbohydrate as well as protein and fibre.

Rassa

CURRIES

JACKFRUIT MASALA

Jackfruit is a truly versatile vegetable, with a wonderful flavour and texture. It's sometimes known as 'vegetarian meat', because it contains lots of fibre. This jackfruit masala is simple and delicious.

500g (1lb 1½oz) unripe jackfruit (fresh or tinned)
2 tablespoons rapeseed oil
250g (9oz) onions, chopped
1 tablespoon Ginger/Garlic Paste (see page 18)
¼ teaspoon ground turmeric
1 teaspoon red chilli powder
½ teaspoon Kashmiri chilli powder
1 teaspoon amchur (dried mango powder)
1 tablespoon ground coriander
150g (5oz) tomatoes, chopped
1 green chilli, deseeded and chopped
1 tablespoon chopped ginger
1 teaspoon Garam Masala (see page 16)
a handful of coriander leaves
salt
chapatis, to serve

If using tinned jackfruit, wash it under running cold water and leave it in a colander. If you are using raw whole jackfruit, first grease your fingers well with vegetable or rapeseed oil, or mustard oil if you have it. Place a bowl of oil next to you while cutting the jackfruit, as you will need to smear your palms with oil from time to time – the oil prevents the jackfruit fibres from sticking to your hand. With a sharp knife remove the skin of the jackfruit and cut out any thick stem in the centre. Cut the jackfruit into small pieces. Don't wash it.

Heat the oil in a kadai or frying pan over a medium heat. Once it starts smoking, add the jackfruit in small batches and shallow-fry until light brown. Remove from the pan, place in a colander and set aside.

Add the onions to the pan and fry until golden brown. Add the Ginger/Garlic Paste and cook for 4–5 minutes, until the raw aroma disappears, then add the turmeric, red chilli powder, dried mango powder, ground coriander and a pinch of salt. Add the tomatoes, green chillies and ginger and cook until the oil separates. This usually takes 5–10 minutes over a low heat.

Add the jackfruit and stir to coat the pieces evenly with the spice mix. Cover with a lid and let the mixture cook over a low heat for 3–4 minutes, stirring occasionally. During this time the jackfruit pieces absorb the flavour of the spices and the sauce should become dry. Sprinkle with the Garam Masala and scatter over the coriander leaves. Serve with chapatis.

GUNCHO KEEMA

Spicy and rich, this cauliflower dish is popular in northern India. People usually make it with cauliflower florets, but here I have grated the cauliflower because I prefer the more minced texture.

30ml (1fl oz) rapeseed oil
1 tablespoon cumin seeds
4 teaspoons chopped garlic
600g (1lb 5oz) cauliflower florets, washed and grated
1 teaspoon red chilli powder
1 teaspoon ground turmeric
120g (4oz) butter
30g (1oz) sweet red peppers, deseeded and diced
30g (1oz) tomatoes, diced
60g (2oz) tomato purée
60g (2oz) khoya (dried milk)
juice of 1 lime
1 teaspoon Garam Masala (see page 16)
1 tablespoon ginger julienne
1 tablespoon chopped coriander leaves
salt

Heat the oil in a lidded pan and add the cumin seeds. Once they start to crackle, add the garlic and sauté for 1 minute. Add the cauliflower, chilli powder, turmeric and a pinch of salt. Mix well, cover the pan, and cook on a low heat for 8–10 minutes.

Meanwhile, melt the butter in another pan and sauté the peppers and tomatoes for 4–5 minutes. Transfer the mixture to the pan with the cauliflower. Add the puréed tomatoes, place on a low heat and cook for a further 5–6 minutes.

Using the same pan you cooked the peppers and tomatoes in, cook the khoya over a very low heat until it becomes granulated. Sprinkle the granulated khoya on top of the cauliflower, add the lime juice and Garam Masala, and garnish with the julienned ginger and chopped coriander.

TIP

If you want to make the dish vegan, replace the dairy with soya cream and vegan butter and do not add the khoya.

LOTUS ROOT KOFTA

Lotus kofta curry is a delicious dish from the Indian subcontinent and is a perfect winter meal. Koftas are fried dumplings made with either vegetables or meat, served in a spicy creamy tomato and onion gravy.

300g (10½oz) lotus stems
150g (5oz) potatoes, boiled and grated
1 tablespoon finely chopped green chillies
2 tablespoons finely chopped
    coriander leaves
1 tablespoon chopped ginger
1 tablespoon dried fenugreek leaves
1 teaspoon amchur (dried mango powder)
½ teaspoon Garam Masala (see page 16)
1 teaspoon red chilli powder
2 tablespoons cornflour, or as needed
200ml (7fl oz) rapeseed oil, for frying
salt
1 tablespoon chopped coriander leaves
chapatis, to serve

FOR THE CURRY

50ml (1¾fl oz) rapeseed oil
2 bay leaves
1 teaspoon cumin seeds
250g (9oz) onions, finely chopped
1 tablespoon Ginger/Garlic Paste
    (see page 18)
½ teaspoon ground turmeric
1 tablespoon ground coriander
1 teaspoon red chilli powder
½ teaspoon Garam Masala (see page 16)
150g (5oz) tomatoes, roughly chopped
1 tablespoon dried fenugreek leaves
50ml (1¾fl oz) double cream

NOTE

Amchur or dried mango powder is made from unripe green mangoes and will add a slightly acidic, citrusy flavour to your dish.

Wash the lotus stems in cold water, then peel and wash again to make sure there is no mud left. Roughly chop, then cook them in boiling salted water for 15–20 minutes. Drain and leave to cool. Once cool, grate.

Put the lotus root, grated potato, green chilli, coriander leaves, ginger, dried fenugreek leaves, dried mango powder, Garam Masala and red chilli powder into a mixing bowl and combine well. Add the cornflour a tablespoon at a time, using just as much as is required to bind the mixture. Season with salt and mix everything well. Divide the mixture into small balls and set aside.

Meanwhile, heat the oil in a pan and add the koftas. Don't add too many at a time, as that will lower the oil temperature and cause the koftas to crumble. When they are golden brown, about 3–4 minutes, flip them over and let the other side cook until they are golden brown all over. Once done, remove them from the pan and drain on kitchen paper. Continue in the same manner until all the koftas are cooked.

To make the curry, heat the oil in a pan and add the bay leaves and cumin seeds. Sauté until they start to change colour, then add the onions and cook until golden brown. Now add the Ginger/Garlic Paste and cook until the raw aroma disappears. Add the turmeric, ground coriander, red chilli powder, dried mango powder, Garam Masala and a little salt and cook for 2–3 minutes.

Blitz the tomatoes in a food processor or blender and add to the pan. Cover and cook on a medium heat for about 2 minutes or until oil starts to appear on the surface. Add 225ml (7½fl oz) water and cook for about 5 minutes.

Crush the fenugreek leaves between your palms and add to the curry. Simmer for 5 minutes, then lower the heat and add the cream slowly, stirring. Add the fried koftas and stir gently.

Garnish with fresh coriander and serve with chapatis.

COURGETTE MUSSALAM

This is a Mughlai dish originating from the Indian subcontinent and was popular among the royal Mughal family of Awadh. If you prefer, this dish can also be made with bottlegourd (louki).

2 courgettes, trimmed and
    halved lengthways

FOR THE FILLING

100g (3½oz) khoya (dried milk), grated
50g (1¾oz) cashews
2 tablespoons rapeseed oil
1 tablespoon chopped ginger
1 tablespoon finely chopped green chillies
250g (9oz) potatoes, boiled and mashed
2 tablespoons chopped coriander leaves
1 tablespoon chopped mint leaves,
    plus extra to garnish
1 teaspoon Garam Masala (see page 16)
¼ teaspoon ground green cardamom
100g (3½oz) Fried Onions (see page 21)
salt

FOR THE GRAVY

2 tablespoons rapeseed oil
1 tablespoon Ginger/Garlic Paste
    (see page 18)
100g (3½oz) Cashew Nut Paste
    (see page 20)
100g (3½oz) Onion Paste (see page 21)
1 teaspoon red chilli powder
¼ teaspoon ground turmeric
50g (1¾oz) yoghurt
1 teaspoon Garam Masala (see page 16)
1 tablespoon dried fenugreek leaves

Scoop the centre out of each half of the courgette, using a corer or a spoon. Heat the oil in a kadai or deep pan to 160°C/320°F, and deep-fry the courgette halves on a medium heat until cooked. Drain on kitchen paper and leave to cool.

To prepare the filling, sauté the khoya in a heavy-based pan until light brown, then remove and set aside. Halve 6–8 cashews and set aside, then roughly chop the rest.

Heat the oil in a pan and add the chopped ginger and green chillies. Sauté for a minute, then add the mashed potatoes, khoya, coriander, mint, chopped cashews, Garam Masala, cardamom and salt to taste and cook for 2–3 minutes.

Transfer the mixture to a plate and leave to cool. Then gently stuff the filling into each piece of fried courgette, pressing it down to ensure it is firmly packed. Set aside.

To prepare the gravy, heat the oil in a pan, add the Ginger/Garlic Paste and cook until the raw aroma disappears. Add the Cashew Nut and Onion Pastes and sauté for 2–3 minutes. Add the red chilli powder and turmeric and continue to sauté for a minute.

Add 225ml (7½fl oz) water, stir, then simmer on a low heat for 2–3 minutes. Add the yoghurt, Garam Masala and salt. Cook on a slow heat until oil starts to appear on top of the gravy. Stir in the fenugreek leaves.

Pour the gravy over the courgettes, garnish with the cashews, mint leaves and serve hot.

KADAI TOFU

Kadai dishes, both vegan and non-vegan, are very popular in India.
It's all about the spice mix, which is made with coriander seeds,
whole red chillies, cumin seeds, fennel seeds and black pepper.
If you don't have a kadai, you can use a wok or really any other pan.

1 tablespoon rapeseed oil
150g (5oz) onions, finely chopped
1 green chilli, sliced
2 teaspoons Ginger/Garlic Paste
    (see page 18)
300g (10½oz) tomatoes, finely chopped
1 tablespoon tomato purée
¼ teaspoon Garam Masala (see page 16)
¾ teaspoon Kashmiri chilli powder
2.5cm (1in) piece of fresh ginger,
    peeled and julienned
2 tablespoons soya cream (optional)
¾ teaspoon salt, or to taste
225g (8oz) tofu, soaked in warm water for
    20–25 minutes, then cubed
1 large green pepper, cut into 2.5cm
    (1in) pieces
1 teaspoon dried fenugreek leaves, crushed
chopped coriander leaves, to garnish
chapatis, to serve

FOR THE MASALA

2 tablespoons coriander seeds
2 dried red chillies (more if you'd like
    the dish hotter)
1 teaspoon cumin seeds
1 teaspoon fennel seeds
½ teaspoon coarsely ground black pepper

First make the masala. In a small kadai or pan, dry roast the spices for 3–4 minutes on a medium heat until fragrant. Remove from the heat and allow to cool slightly, then grind half to a fine powder and leave the other half coarse. Set both aside.

Heat the oil in a pan that you can subsequently cover with a lid and add the coarse masala. Stir, then add the onions and sauté until golden brown. Add the green chilli and the Ginger/Garlic Paste and sauté for a further 1–2 minutes.

Add the tomatoes and tomato purée, stir, then cook for around 6 minutes until the tomatoes are really soft. Add 3–4 teaspoons of the fine masala (or add all of it if you like it spicy). Stir in the Garam Masala and Kashmiri chilli powder.

Add half the julienned ginger, cook for 30 seconds, then stir in 120ml (4fl oz) water. Add the soya cream (if using) and salt, and mix well. Cook for 1 minute.

Add the tofu and green pepper and mix well. Cover the pan with a lid and cook for 5–6 minutes on a medium heat until the pepper has softened slightly. Stir in the dried fenugreek leaves, along with the remaining julienned ginger and garnish with the coriander. Serve with chapatis.

KADHI PAKORA

Tangy and flavourful, these deep-fried pakoras (fritters)
are simmered in a tangy yoghurt and gram flour based curry.
Each region has its own kadhi, but the most famous is
Punjabi kadhi pakora. This is my simple and quick recipe,
which I like to serve with plain rice.

250g (9oz) besan (gram flour)
500g (1lb 1½oz) natural yoghurt
4 tablespoons rapeseed oil
10–12 fresh curry leaves
½ teaspoon cumin seeds
1 teaspoon mustard seeds
1 tablespoon Ginger/Garlic Paste
   (see page 18)
2–3 green chillies, slit down one side
1 teaspoon ground turmeric
a pinch of asafoetida
1 teaspoon Kashmiri chilli powder
1 teaspoon Garam Masala (see page 16)
1 tablespoon dried fenugreek leaves
salt
rice or roti, to serve

FOR THE PAKORAS

50g (1¾oz) besan (gram flour)
1 green chilli, chopped
½ teaspoon ground turmeric
¼ teaspoon baking powder
oil, for deep-frying

FOR THE TADKA

2 tablespoons rapeseed oil
1 teaspoon mustard seeds
8–10 fresh curry leaves
2–3 red chillies
3 garlic cloves, finely chopped
¼ teaspoon Kashmiri chilli powder

To make the kadhi sauce, put the gram flour and yoghurt into a mixing bowl with 350ml (12fl oz) water and whisk until smooth.

Heat the oil in a large pan. Add the curry leaves, cumin seeds and mustard seeds, and once they start to crackle add the Ginger/Garlic Paste and cook until the raw aroma disappears. Add the green chillies, turmeric, asafoetida, Kashmiri chilli powder and some salt, and mix well.

Add the gram flour and yoghurt mixture and bring to the boil. Add the Garam Masala, then put the lid on and cook on a low heat for about 1–1½ hours, stirring regularly.

To make the pakoras, put the gram flour, green chilli, turmeric, baking powder and a pinch of salt into a medium bowl and mix well. Gradually add water, stirring to form a smooth and thick batter.

Heat the oil in a deep pan, then drop in spoonfuls of the pakora mixture and fry until golden and crispy. Transfer the fried pakoras to the kadhi sauce and cook on a medium heat for about 8 minutes or so.

To make the tadka, heat the oil in a frying pan and add the mustard seeds, curry leaves and red chillies. Once they start to crackle, add the garlic and fry for a few seconds. Add the chilli powder and mix well.

Now pour the tadka on top of the kadhi pakora and serve with rice or roti.

MUSHROOM AND TRUFFLE KHICHADI

As a child, I would demand that my mum make me khichadi almost
every day for lunch. Those were simpler days! At Kutir, I serve
a version made with wild mushrooms and fresh truffle, which has
become one of my signature dishes and is very popular. Here,
I have adapted it so you can make it at home. *Pictured overleaf.*

200g (7oz) basmati rice
300g (10½oz) toor dal (yellow split peas)
2 tablespoons vegetable oil
1 bay leaf
½ teaspoon cumin seeds
½ teaspoon grated ginger
a pinch of asafoetida
100g (3½oz) onions, chopped
1 green chilli, slit down one side
100g (3½oz) tomatoes, chopped
a pinch of ground turmeric
salt

FOR THE MUSHROOMS

2 tablespoons vegetable oil
500g (1lb 1½oz) mushrooms (a mix
    of wild or cultivated), chopped
1 teaspoon cumin seeds
100g (3½oz) onions, finely chopped
1 tablespoon Ginger/Garlic Paste
    (see page 18)
¼ teaspoon ground turmeric
1 tablespoon ground coriander
½ teaspoon Kashmiri chilli powder
½ teaspoon Garam Masala (see page 16)
100g (3½oz) tomatoes, chopped

TO GARNISH

1 teaspoon truffle oil
2 teaspoons fresh black truffle,
    shaved or grated
1 tablespoon chopped coriander leaves

NOTE

This is delicious served with
poppadums, along with some
chutneys and pickles on the side.

CONTINUED OVERLEAF

Wash the rice and lentils at least three times in fresh water, then drain well and set aside.

Heat the oil in a large saucepan set on a medium heat, and add the bay leaf and cumin seeds. Cook for 1 minute, then add the grated ginger and cook until fragrant. Add the asafoetida, followed by the onions and green chilli, and cook for about 5 minutes until the onions have softened.

Add the tomatoes, turmeric and a large pinch of salt and cook for 3–4 minutes. Add the drained rice and lentils and give it a good stir. Add 750ml (1 pint 9fl oz) water for a thick consistency, or, if you prefer a looser, porridge-like khichadi, add 1 litre (2 pints) water. Stir once, check for seasoning, then leave to simmer, giving the mixture the occasional stir, while you cook the mushrooms. If the mixture begins to stick, add a little more water.

To cook the mushrooms, heat 1 tablespoon of the oil in a non-stick frying pan over a medium heat. Add the mushrooms in batches with a large pinch of salt and cook until they are golden brown all over and most of the moisture has evaporated.

Meanwhile, place another frying pan over a medium heat and add the remaining tablespoon of oil. Add the cumin seeds and once they begin to crackle, add the onions and cook until they are caramelised, crisp and golden brown. Add the Ginger/Garlic Paste, cook for a few minutes, then add the turmeric, coriander, chilli powder and Garam Masala. Cook gently for 4–5 minutes, then add the tomatoes and simmer for about 10 minutes until they are soft. Add the caramelised mushrooms, give everything a good mix and remove from the heat.

By this time the khichadi should be ready – it should take 20–25 minutes. Taste a spoonful of the rice and lentils to ensure they're cooked through.

To serve, divide the rice between bowls and top with the mushroom mixture. Drizzle with truffle oil, generously cover with shaved or grated truffle and garnish with coriander.

BAINGAN KA BHARTA

This aubergine dish is known all over India and southern Asia and comes from the Punjab. The aubergine is cooked over a flame, which gives it a smoky flavour, but you can also roast it in the oven. Serve with phulkas or roti, along with dal, or you can treat it as a side dish.

2 large aubergines
50ml (1¾fl oz) rapeseed oil,
    plus extra for the aubergines
200g (7oz) onions, finely chopped
5–6 garlic cloves, finely chopped
2 green chillies, finely chopped
25g (1oz) fresh ginger, finely chopped
150g (5oz) tomatoes, finely chopped
¼ teaspoon red chilli powder
1 tablespoon ground coriander
½ teaspoon Garam Masala (see page 16)
½ teaspoon Kashmiri chilli powder
    or red chilli powder
100g (3½oz) frozen green peas
1 tablespoon chopped coriander leaves
salt

Rinse the aubergines, pat dry, then rub them all over with oil. Using tongs, hold the aubergines one at a time over a gas flame until the skin blackens and the flesh is tender and soft, turning after 2–3 minutes to ensure that they are evenly cooked on both sides. When cool enough to handle, peel off the skins and either chop the flesh or mash it in a bowl.

Pour the oil into a kadai or other medium pan and set on a medium heat. When hot, add the onions and garlic and sauté until the onions are golden brown. Stir in the green chillies and ginger, followed by the tomatoes. Let cook, stirring often, until the tomatoes are soft and the oil begins to separate.

Add the ground spices, mix well and cook for 5–6 minutes. Add the aubergine pulp and green peas, mixing them in well. Season to taste with salt and cook, stirring often, for a further 4–5 minutes. Stir in the coriander leaves and serve.

DUM ALOO

This is a potato-based dish that is part of the traditional Kashmiri Pandit cuisine, from the Kashmir Valley, in the Indian state of Jammu and Kashmir. The potatoes, usually smaller ones, are deep-fried, then cooked slowly on a low heat in a gravy with spices.

12 baby potatoes
300ml (10fl oz) rapeseed oil
300g (10½oz) Greek yoghurt
2 tablespoons Kashmiri chilli powder
1 tablespoon ground ginger
1 teaspoon ground fennel seed
¼ teaspoon ground mace
⅓ teaspoon ground green cardamom
1 tablespoon ground coriander
2 bay leaves
a pinch of asafoetida
1 tablespoon Ginger/Garlic Paste
   (see page 18)
½ teaspoon ground turmeric
50g (1¾oz) puréed fresh tomatoes
4 green chillies, deseeded and slit
   down one side
½ teaspoon Garam Masala (see page 16)
1 tablespoon dried fenugreek leaves
1 tablespoon chopped coriander leaves
salt
parathas or naan, to serve

Peel the potatoes and prick them with a fork. If small potatoes are not available, use larger potatoes cut into chunks. Wash and dry the potatoes.

Heat the oil (setting 4 tablespoons aside for later) to 170°C/340°F in a kadai or a pan suitable for deep frying. Deep-fry the potatoes on a medium heat until golden brown, about 8–10 minutes. Drain and transfer to a plate.

Put the yoghurt in a mixing bowl and add the Kashmiri chilli powder, ground ginger, fennel seed, mace, cardamom and ground coriander and a pinch of salt. Mix together with a whisk or fork to make a smooth paste, then set aside.

Heat the reserved oil in another pan. Add the bay leaves and asafoetida and sauté for 30 seconds. Add the Ginger/Garlic Paste and cook for 3–4 minutes, until the raw aroma disappears. Add the turmeric and puréed tomatoes and cook until the oil starts to separate. Add 250ml (8½fl oz) water, bring to the boil and add the yoghurt.

Bring the mixture back to the boil and add the fried potatoes and green chillies and the Garam Masala. Cook on a medium heat until the potatoes have absorbed the gravy and the oil starts to come to the surface, about 10 minutes. Finish with the dried fenugreek, then turn off the heat.

Garnish with chopped coriander and serve with parathas or naan.

PANEER ANARDANA

Paneer anardana is a rich dish of deep-fried stuffed paneer in
a smooth, flavourful, creamy onion and tomato-based gravy.
This is a restaurant-style recipe that you can easily make at home.

1 tablespoon Raw Mango Chutney
   (see page 171)
2 tablespoons finely chopped cashews
1 teaspoon finely chopped green chillies
2 tablespoons chopped coriander leaves
½ tablespoon chopped mint leaves
½ teaspoon red chilli powder
1 teaspoon pomegranate powder
½ teaspoon toasted ground cumin
250g (9oz) paneer
250ml (8½fl oz) rapeseed oil, for frying
salt

FOR THE GRAVY

150g (5oz) Fried Onions (see page 21)
100g (3½oz) cashews, toasted or fried
2 tablespoons yoghurt
2 tablespoons rapeseed oil
1 bay leaf
½ teaspoon black cumin seeds

1 tablespoon Ginger/Garlic Paste
   (see page 18)
¼ teaspoon ground turmeric
1 teaspoon ground coriander
1 teaspoon Kashmiri chilli powder
200g (7oz) tomatoes, blitzed in a blender
1 tablespoon kewra water (see page 206)
½ teaspoon Garam Masala (see page 16)
1 teaspoon crushed dried fenugreek leaves
2 tablespoons double cream
2 tablespoons chopped coriander leaves,
   to garnish
2 tablespoons pomegranate seeds,
   to garnish
naan, roti or chapatis, to serve

FOR THE BATTER

3 tablespoons cornflour
2 tablespoons rice flour
1 teaspoon ground turmeric

Put the Raw Mango Chutney, cashews, green chillies, chopped coriander and mint leaves, red chilli powder, pomegranate powder, toasted ground cumin and a little salt into a bowl. Mix everything together and set aside.

Cut the paneer into triangles. Make a slit in each triangle of paneer and gently place some of the stuffing inside the slits, using a small knife. Set the stuffed pieces aside.

Heat the oil to 170°C/340°F in a deep pan. Make a batter by mixing the cornflour, rice flour, turmeric and a little salt in a bowl. Add just enough water to make a smooth batter (it should be just thick enough to coat the paneer pieces and hold the stuffing inside). Dip the stuffed paneer into the batter, or use a spoon or small tongs to coat the pieces. Fry them in the hot oil, turning them around until they are golden brown on all sides, about 3–4 minutes.

Drain the fried paneer on kitchen paper and set aside.

To make the gravy, put the Fried Onions, cashews and yoghurt into a food processor or blender with a little water and grind to a smooth paste. Set aside.

Heat the oil in a pan and add the bay leaf and black cumin seeds. Sauté until the seeds start to crackle, then add the Ginger/Garlic Paste. Stir and sauté until the raw aroma of the garlic goes away. Add the turmeric, ground coriander, a little salt and Kashmiri chilli powder, stir well, then add the blended tomatoes. Stir and cook for 3–4 minutes on a low-medium heat, then add the fried onion paste and cook for another 3–4 minutes.

Add 200ml (7fl oz) water and cook on a low heat for about 10–15 minutes. If the gravy spits, cover the pan with a lid. When specks of oil start to appear on the surface, it is ready. Check the seasoning and add the kewra water, Garam Masala, dried fenugreek leaves and cream, stirring until the cream is mixed in evenly.

To serve, either put the fried paneer pieces into the gravy or place them on a serving plate and pour the gravy over the top.

Serve hot, garnished with coriander leaves and pomegranate seeds, along with naan, roti or chapatis.

BHARLELI VANGI

Aubergine curry recipes are common, in fact, each state and region of India has its own variation. One hugely popular Maharashtrian version is this spicy curry. *Pictured overleaf.*

9 small aubergines
2 tablespoons finely chopped coriander,
    to serve

FOR THE MASALA STUFFING

60g (2oz) peanuts, skinless
1 teaspoon ground cumin
2 tablespoons sesame seeds
3 tablespoons desiccated coconut
¼ teaspoon ground turmeric
1 teaspoon red chilli powder
1 tablespoon Goda Masala (see page 17)
½ teaspoon salt
2–3 garlic cloves, chopped
1 tablespoon chopped fresh ginger
1 tablespoon tamarind paste (see page 35)
3 tablespoons ground coriander

FOR THE CURRY

4 tablespoons oil
1 teaspoon mustard seeds
½ teaspoon poppy seeds
a pinch of asafoetida
200g (7oz) onions, finely chopped
1 tablespoon Ginger/Garlic Paste
    (see page 18)
¼ teaspoon ground turmeric
½ teaspoon red chilli powder
1 teaspoon Kashmiri chilli powder
100g (3½oz) tomatoes, finely chopped
salt

Slit each aubergine down the centre and across, but not all the way through. Put them into water to prevent discolouring.

To make the stuffing, toast the peanuts in a dry frying pan on a low heat. Add the cumin, sesame and coconut and toast for a couple of minutes until the coconut turns golden brown. Transfer to a plate and leave to cool.

Put the toasted mixture in a food processor or blender with the turmeric, chilli powder, Goda Masala, salt, garlic, ginger, tamarind and ground coriander and blend to a coarse paste without adding water. Stuff about 1 teaspoon of this masala into each aubergine and set aside. Reserve the rest of the masala.

To prepare the curry, heat 2 tablespoons of the oil in a large kadai or pan on a medium heat and add the mustard seeds, poppy seeds and asafoetida. Once the seeds start crackling, add the onions and cook until they turn golden. Add the Ginger/Garlic Paste and continue to cook on a low heat. Add the turmeric, chilli powder and a pinch of salt and sauté until the spices turn aromatic.

Add the reserved masala stuffing mixture and sauté for 2 minutes. Add the tomatoes and cook until they are soft. Now add the stuffed aubergines to the pan and cook for 2 minutes, without breaking them up. Add 250ml (8½fl oz) water and mix gently, then cover the pan and cook for 10 minutes, or until the aubergines are cooked through.

Stir in the coriander and serve with chapatis.

BOTTLEGOURD KOFTA

Lauki ke kofte are fried, spicy dumplings cooked in an onion and tomato gravy. I remember when I was a kid I always refused to eat bottlegourd, but my mum made it into koftas and I fell in love.

750g (1lb 10½oz) bottlegourd, washed, peeled and coarsely grated
200g (7oz) besan (gram flour)
½ teaspoon red chilli powder
¼ teaspoon ground turmeric
1 teaspoon amchur (dried mango powder)
1 tablespoon chopped fresh ginger
2 green chillies, deseeded and chopped
rapeseed oil, for frying
salt
1 tablespoon chopped coriander leaves, to serve
chapatis, to serve

FOR THE GRAVY

75ml (2½fl oz) rapeseed oil
1 teaspoon cumin seeds
2 bay leaves
350g (12¼oz) onions, chopped
1 tablespoon Ginger/Garlic Paste (see page 18)
1 tablespoon ground coriander
1 teaspoon ground turmeric
1 teaspoon red chilli powder
150g (5oz) tomatoes, chopped
1 tablespoon dried fenugreek leaves
1 teaspoon Garam Masala (see page 16)

Tightly squeeze out all the liquid from the bottlegourd – don't leave out this step or the whole mixture will become runny and difficult to handle. Transfer it to a big bowl. Add the rest of the ingredients apart from the oil, then gradually add a little water at a time, mixing well until thick and firm enough to shape into dumplings.

Heat the oil in a kadai or pan on a medium heat. Oil your hands, then take tablespoons of the mixture and roll them into balls between your palms. Drop them into the hot oil and fry until golden brown. Place on kitchen paper and set aside.

To make the gravy, heat the oil in a pan on a medium heat. Add the cumin seeds and bay leaves, and once they start to crackle, add the onions and cook until they start turning light golden brown. Add the Ginger/Garlic Paste and cook for couple of minutes until the raw aroma of the garlic disappears, adding a few drops of water if it starts to stick to the pan.

Add the ground coriander, turmeric and chilli powder and cook for 2–3 minutes. Add the tomatoes and stir well until they are soft. Add 300ml (10fl oz) water and leave the gravy on a low heat for 8–10 minutes, depending on how thick you prefer it to be. If you don't like the chunky texture of onion and tomatoes in gravy, take it off the heat, let cool, then blitz it using a hand blender – it will thicken in consistency.

Adjust the seasoning, add the dried fenugreek and Garam Masala and return the pan to the heat. Add the koftas to the gravy and cook for 2–3 minutes. Remove from the heat and let the koftas soak in the hot gravy for 10–15 minutes.

Garnish with chopped coriander and serve hot with chapatis.

KHUBANI SOYA KEEMA

This is the vegan version of the popular Indian minced meat curry called keema. You cook it the same way as meat, but soya is rather tasteless on its own, so you need to spice it up a little. Here I've cooked it with apricots and whole spices to increase the flavour and taste.

150g (5oz) soya mince
4 tablespoons rapeseed oil
4 cloves
a small piece of cinnamon stick
4 green cardamom pods, seeds crushed
1 black cardamom
2 bay leaves
150g (5oz) onions, finely chopped,
    plus extra to garnish
2 tablespoons Garlic/Ginger Paste
    (see page 18)
100g (3½oz) tomatoes, chopped
1 tablespoon ground coriander
1 teaspoon ground turmeric
1 teaspoon ground cumin
1 tablespoon Garam Masala (see page 16)
½ teaspoon red chilli powder
1 teaspoon Kashmiri chilli powder
8–10 dried apricots, cut into small pieces
1 tablespoon soya cream (optional)
1 tablespoon dried fenugreek leaves
a handful of chopped coriander leaves
salt
hot buttered buns, to serve

Soak the soya mince in water for about 15–20 minutes. Meanwhile, heat the oil in a heavy-based pan on a medium heat and add the cloves, cinnamon, cardamom and bay leaves. When the spices start to crackle, add the onions and cook until they start to turn golden brown. Add the Garlic/ Ginger Paste and stir-fry until the raw aroma disappears.

Add the tomatoes and continue to cook on a medium heat. Add the ground spices, apricots and a pinch of salt. You can add 2 tablespoons water if the mixture begins to stick to the base of the pan. Continue to stir-fry for another 5 minutes.

Drain the soya mince and add to the pan. Mix well and cook for 10–12 minutes, stirring regularly, until the mince is dark brown. Check the seasoning and finish with the soya cream (if using) and the dried fenugreek leaves.

Scatter over the coriander leaves and serve with hot buttered buns and chopped onions.

PANEER MAKHANI

In this delicious curry, paneer is cooked in a buttery tomato gravy
flavoured with fenugreek leaves. It's very popular in Punjab as well
as in northern India. Paneer makhani goes well with roti and naan.
It's also known as paneer makhanwala. My kids love it.

100ml (3½fl oz) rapeseed oil
1kg (2lb) tomatoes, roughly chopped
2 tablespoons Kashmiri chilli powder
50g (1¾oz) ginger, roughly chopped
30g (1oz) garlic, roughly chopped
5 green cardamom pods
2–3 green chillies, roughly chopped
3–4 bay leaves
1 tablespoon cumin seeds
2 blades of mace
150g (5oz) unsalted butter
2½ tablespoons Ginger/Garlic Paste
    (see page 18)
1 tablespoon crushed dried
    fenugreek leaves
2 tablespoons honey
1 teaspoon Garam Masala (see page 16)
300g (10½oz) paneer, cut into cubes
150ml (5fl oz) double cream
2 tablespoons chopped coriander leaves
1 tablespoon ginger julienne
salt
roti or naan, to serve

Heat the oil to 170°C/340°F in a deep pan
on a medium heat and add the tomatoes,
half the Kashmiri chilli powder, the ginger
and garlic, green cardamoms, green chillies,
bay leaves, cumin seeds, mace and a pinch
of salt. Add 450ml (15fl oz) water and cook
until the tomatoes are fully broken down,
then remove from the heat and set aside to
cool. Once cool, blend the mixture in a food
processor or blender, then put through
a fine sieve.

Heat the butter in a pan on a medium
heat, add the Ginger/Garlic Paste and
cook until the raw aroma disappears. Add
the remaining Kashmiri chilli powder and
the blended tomato mixture and cook on
a low heat for about 30 minutes or until
the consistency of double cream. Add the
fenugreek leaves and mix well. Check and
adjust the seasoning, then add the honey
and Garam Masala and cook for a further
minute, stirring continuously.

Add the paneer pieces to the pan and cook
for 5 minutes. Finally, add the cream, mix
well and turn off the heat.

Garnish with the chopped coriander and
julienned ginger, and serve with roti or naan.

BAINGAN MIRCH KA SALAN

Baingan mirch ka salan is a traditional Hyderabadi curry.
A combination of green chillies and aubergines cooked in a
coconut, peanut and sesame seed curry, it's usually served with
Hyderabadi biryani, but it can be served with plain rice or roti, too.

3 tablespoons rapeseed oil,
    plus extra for deep-frying
10 baby aubergines
3 large green chillies, such as Padrón
1 large onion, chopped
8–10 curry leaves
1 teaspoon cumin seeds
½ teaspoon mustard seeds
1 teaspoon nigella seeds
1 teaspoon Ginger/Garlic Paste
    (see page 18)
3 tablespoons tamarind paste
    (see page 35)
½ teaspoon ground turmeric
1 teaspoon red chilli powder
salt

FOR THE MASALA

120g (4oz) sesame seeds
2 tablespoons poppy seeds
2–3 dried red chillies
2 tablespoons coriander seeds
1 teaspoon fenugreek seeds
120g (4oz) peanuts
60g (2oz) freshly grated
    or desiccated coconut

Heat the oil for deep-frying to 160°C/320°F
in a large pan. Cut a slit in each aubergine,
lengthways and across, but not all the way
through, and cut a slit down one side of
each chilli. Deep-fry the aubergines and
chillies until cooked through. Set aside.

To make the masala, dry roast the sesame
seeds, poppy seeds, dried chillies, coriander
seeds, fenugreek seeds, peanuts and
coconut in a small pan until lightly browned.
Remove to a bowl. Once the mixture cools
slightly, add enough water to grind them to
a smooth paste.

Heat 1 tablespoon of the oil in the same
pan and sauté the onions until lightly
browned. Remove from the pan and grind
to a smooth paste.

Heat the remaining oil in a second pan and
add the curry leaves, cumin seeds, mustard
seeds and nigella seeds and once they
start to crackle, add the onion paste. Cook
for 1–2 minutes, so that the paste absorbs
the flavours.

Add the Ginger/Garlic Paste and cook for
1 minute. Then add the masala and cook,
covered, for 3–4 minutes.

Add the tamarind paste, turmeric, chilli
powder, some salt and the sautéed
aubergines and chillies along with
500–750ml (1 pint–1 pint 9fl oz) water.
Mix well. Lower the heat to medium-
low, then cover the pan and cook for
20–25 minutes, or until the vegetables
are completely cooked through and the
gravy is thick.

Dal
&
Sabzi

SIDE DISHES

CARROT KOSHAMBIR

This easy, quick and healthy salad comes from southern India.
It's delicious for lunch or as a snack between meals. It could
be served with grilled veggies or as a side dish.

2 carrots, julienned or grated
50g (1¾oz) mixed beansprouts
5cm (2in) piece of fresh turmeric, julienned
½ small green mango, julienned

FOR TEMPERING

2 tablespoons rapeseed oil
1 teaspoon mustard seeds
1 tablespoon urad dal (split black gram)
30g (1oz) toasted skinless crushed
   peanuts (optional)
5–6 curry leaves, chopped
a pinch of asafoetida
2 tablespoons lime juice
30g (1oz) fresh grated coconut
1 tablespoon chopped coriander leaves
salt

Put all the salad ingredients into a mixing bowl, mix well and set aside.

Heat the oil for tempering in a hot pan and add the mustard seeds. Once they begin to crackle and pop, add the split black gram, crushed peanuts (if using), curry leaves and asafoetida. Pour this over the salad mixture. Add the lime juice, salt, fresh coconut and chopped coriander. Mix well and serve either at room temperature or cold.

NOTE

The cutting technique known as julienne is for when you slice the ingredient into thin matchstick-like pieces. If your knife skills aren't brilliant, do use a grater here.

JEERA ALOO

Jeera aloo is one of the most popular Indian dishes. It's vegan, and easy to make using a handful of basic ingredients. Most Indian travellers carry poori with jeera aloo when they're travelling, because it is easy to handle and has a long shelf life. This is great served with pooris, parathas or as a side dish with dal and rice.

500g (1lb 1½oz) potatoes
2 tablespoons rapeseed oil
1 tablespoon cumin seeds
2 green chillies, finely chopped
1 tablespoon finely chopped ginger
½ teaspoon ground turmeric
1 tablespoon ground coriander
¼ teaspoon red chilli powder, or to taste
a generous pinch of asafoetida
2 tablespoons chopped coriander leaves
1 tablespoon lemon juice
salt

Cook the potatoes in boiling salted water until tender, making sure they don't overcook or break up. Once drained and cooled, peel the potatoes and cut them into cubes. Set aside.

Heat the oil in a pan on a medium heat, then add the cumin seeds and let them sizzle. Immediately lower the heat so that they don't burn. Add the green chillies and ginger, ground spices and asafoetida and sauté for a few seconds.

Add the boiled and cubed potatoes to the pan and toss with the spices. Let the potatoes cook for 2–3 minutes on a medium heat, then mix in the chopped coriander. Check the seasoning and add the lemon juice to finish.

JAIPURI BHINDI

This is an easy, quick and delicious dish from Rajasthani cuisine. These fritters of okra are usually enjoyed as an evening snack or a side dish – I like to serve them with dal and rice as a main.

500g (1lb 1½oz) okra, washed, dried and finely sliced
1 tablespoon Ginger/Garlic Paste (see page 18)
1 tablespoon chopped green chilli
1 tablespoon chopped ginger
1 teaspoon red chilli powder
1 teaspoon ground coriander
1 tablespoon amchur (dried mango powder)
½ teaspoon ground turmeric
¼ teaspoon asafoetida
4 tablespoons besan (gram flour)
1 tablespoon rice flour
1 tablespoon lemon juice
300ml (10fl oz) rapeseed oil, for deep-frying
salt

Place the okra in a large mixing bowl and add the Ginger/Garlic Paste, chilli, ginger, all the ground spices and a little salt to taste. Mix together gently.

Sprinkle the gram flour and rice flour on top of the okra mixture and add the lemon juice and a little water if needed. The idea is that the okra should be coated evenly with the spices and flour.

Heat the oil to 170°C/340°F in a deep pan or kadai over a medium heat, and once it is hot enough, drop in spoonfuls of the okra mixture and deep-fry like fritters until crisp about 3–4 minutes. Serve hot.

KWATI

Kwati, a traditional Nepalese dish, is a mix of nine beans and pulses and is eaten as part of a celebration during the full moon festival. I discovered this recipe when I went to Nepal for research – Nepalese cuisine has so much depth and offers great variety for both vegetarian and vegan diets.

1 tablespoon whole black gram
1 tablespoon dried green peas
1 tablespoon chana dal (split chickpeas)
1 tablespoon chickpeas
1 tablespoon kidney beans
1 tablespoon black-eyed beans
1 tablespoon soya beans
1 tablespoon whole green lentils
50ml (1¾fl oz) mustard oil
¼ teaspoon ajwain (carom seeds)
4 garlic cloves
2 dried red chillies
4–5 cloves
3 x 5cm (2in) pieces of cinnamon stick
100g (3½oz) onions, chopped
1 teaspoon roasted ground cumin
½ teaspoon red chilli powder
¼ teaspoon ground turmeric
1 tablespoon ground coriander
50g (1¾oz) tomatoes, chopped
½ teaspoon Garam Masala (see page 16)
1 tablespoon clarified butter
1 tablespoon chopped coriander leaves,
    to garnish
salt

First clean all the lentils and soak them overnight in water. Next day, put them into a pan and cover them with water. Cook them for 3–4 hours until tender, then drain and set aside.

Heat the mustard oil in a pan and add the ajwain, garlic, red chillies, cloves and cinnamon. When the seeds start to crackle, add the chopped onions and cook until golden brown. Add the ground cumin, chilli powder, turmeric, ground coriander and a pinch of salt. Mix well, then fry for 5 minutes.

Add the tomatoes and cook for another 2–3 minutes, then add all the boiled lentils and mix well. Add water if required, and cook for another 10 minutes on a slow heat until you reach the desired consistency, depending upon your preference.

Add the Garam Masala and butter and serve hot, sprinkled with coriander.

BRUSSELS SPROUT PORIYAL

This is a very simple, quick and healthy dish. Poriyal is a simple stir-fry from southern Indian cuisine, which is mostly prepared to accompany rice, along with sambhar. But it also goes well with chapatis or roti. A poriyal can be made with any vegetables, for example carrots, beans, asparagus, broccoli, cabbage or even peas. Here I am using Brussels sprouts, my favourite version.

250g (9oz) Brussels sprouts, trimmed and halved
1 tablespoon rapeseed oil
1 teaspoon mustard seeds
1 teaspoon urad dal (split black gram)
1 dried red chilli
a pinch of asafoetida
1 sprig of curry leaves
100g (3½oz) onions, sliced
1 tablespoon chopped ginger
1 tablespoon chopped green chilli
½ teaspoon ground turmeric
½ teaspoon red chilli powder
1 tablespoon chopped coriander leaves
3 tablespoons grated fresh coconut
salt

Blanch the Brussels sprouts for a few minutes in boiling water with a little salt added. Remove from the water and put them into a colander under cold running water for a few more minutes. Set aside to cool.

Heat the oil in a pan on a medium heat, and add the mustard seeds, urad dal and dried red chilli. When the dal turns golden, add the asafoetida and curry leaves and fry until the leaves turn crisp. Add the sliced onions and cook until they start to turn golden brown. Add the ginger, green chilli, ground turmeric and red chilli powder and mix well.

Add the blanched Brussels sprouts along with a pinch of salt and sauté for 2 minutes. Cover and cook for another 2–3 minutes on a low heat. This helps to release the moisture. If needed, you can sprinkle with 1–2 tablespoons water. Cover and cook until the sprouts are soft and tender. Add the chopped coriander and grated coconut, mix well and sauté for a further minute. Turn off the heat and serve the poriyal with plain rice.

ALOO GOBI

Aloo gobi is a popular Indian dish in which potatoes and cauliflower are cooked with onions, tomatoes and spices. You can also make it just with onions, or just with tomatoes, or you can use no onions and tomatoes at all. This recipe is packed with flavours, is vegan and is simply the best aloo gobi you will ever eat!

4 teaspoons rapeseed oil
1 cauliflower, cut into small florets
2 potatoes, diced
½ teaspoon cumin seeds
1 onion, chopped
1½ teaspoons Ginger/Garlic Paste
    (see page 18)
2 tomatoes, chopped
½ teaspoon ground turmeric
¼ teaspoon red chilli powder
1 teaspoon ground coriander
½ teaspoon amchur (dried mango powder)
2 tablespoons chopped coriander leaves,
    plus extra leaves to serve
¼ teaspoon Garam Masala (see page 16)
salt

Heat 2 teaspoons of the oil in a pan on a medium heat. Add the cauliflower florets and fry for 2–3 minutes, then add the potatoes. Fry on a medium-low heat for 7–8 minutes, until the potatoes and cauliflower are starting to get a few brown spots on them. Drain on kitchen paper and set aside.

In the same pan, heat the remaining oil on a medium heat, then add the cumin seeds and once they start to crackle, add the onions and cook for 2 minutes, until translucent. Add the Ginger/Garlic Paste and cook for another 2 minutes, or until the raw aroma disappears. Add the tomatoes and cook for 2 minutes until they are soft. Add the turmeric, red chilli powder, ground coriander and dried mango powder.

Cover the pan and let the mixture cook for 2–3 minutes, then add the potatoes and cauliflower. Add the chopped coriander and give it a good mix. Stir in the Garam Masala and cook on a medium-low heat for 5–6 minutes. Season with salt, then cover the pan and cook for another 6–7 minutes on a low heat, until the potatoes and cauliflower are tender.

Sprinkle with coriander leaves and serve hot, with any Indian bread.

DAL MAKHANI

One of the most popular dishes and everyone's favourite, dal makhani is made with whole black lentils and split chana lentils cooked with butter and cream and simmered on a low heat for that unique flavour. I always prefer dal makhani with garlic naan or plain pulao. Back home my mum makes different dals every day, like toor dal (yellow split peas), masoor dal (red lentils) and chana dal. But she makes this only on special occasions. *Pictured overleaf.*

100g (3½oz) sabut urad (whole black gram)
25g (1oz) chana dal (split chickpeas)
1 tablespoon Kashmiri chilli powder
1 tablespoon Ginger/Garlic Paste (see page 18)
50g (1¾oz) salted butter
1 tablespoon vegetable oil
75g (2½oz) tomato purée or blended fresh tomatoes
1 teaspoon Garam Masala (see page 16)
50g (1¾oz) double cream
1 teaspoon crushed dried fenugreek leaves
salt

Pick over and wash the black gram and split chana lentils, then soak overnight in plenty of cold water. Drain.

Put the drained black gram and chana lentils into a pan with 750ml (1 pint 9fl oz) water. Add a pinch of salt and half the Kashmiri chilli powder (you can also add half the Ginger/Garlic Paste if you wish), and cook until soft about 25–30 minutes. Alternatively, you can cook the dal in a pressure cooker following the maker's instructions.

Heat half the butter and the oil in a pan and add the Ginger/Garlic Paste (or the remaining half if you added half to the lentils earlier) and sauté until golden. Add the tomato purée and sauté on a high heat. Add the rest of the chilli powder and sauté until the tomato is reduced and cooked.

Add the cooked dal. If the mixture is too thick, add water, a little at a time, until it reaches the right consistency. Add the Garam Masala and adjust the salt, then simmer on a low heat until the dals are totally soft and well blended.

Finish with the rest of the butter, the cream and the crushed dried fenugreek leaves.

PALAK PANEER

This is a simple, easy and quick recipe. Palak paneer is a popular
Indian dish in which paneer is cooked with spinach purée, but
I use half the spinach puréed and the other half chopped, for
a variety of texture. My daughters eat this at least twice a week.

350g (12¼oz) fresh spinach leaves
1 tablespoon rapeseed oil
1 tablespoon cumin seeds
100g (3½oz) onions, finely chopped
5 garlic cloves, finely chopped
1 tablespoon finely chopped ginger
1 green chilli, finely chopped
½ teaspoon red chilli powder
¼ teaspoon ground turmeric
100g (3½oz) tomatoes, finely chopped
1 teaspoon Garam Masala (see page 16)
1 tablespoon dried fenugreek leaves
225g (8oz) paneer, cut into cubes
2 tablespoons double cream
1 tablespoon lemon juice
salt
naan or roti, to serve

Blanch the spinach leaves for 2–3 minutes, until wilted, then take them out of the pan and put them into ice-cold water. This helps the leaves retain their green colour. Take half the blanched spinach and purée it in a blender. Chop the rest and set aside.

Heat the oil in a pan and add the cumin seeds. Once they start to crackle, add the onions and cook until they start to turn golden brown. Add the garlic, ginger and green chilli, stir well, and cook for another 2–3 minutes. Add the red chilli powder and turmeric, then stir in the tomatoes and cook until soft.

Add the chopped and puréed spinach and cook for a couple of minutes, stirring. Add about 125ml (4¼fl oz) water, then cover the pan and let the mixture cook for 5 minutes on a medium heat. The spinach will bubble a lot. Stir it regularly to prevent it sticking to the pan.

Add the Garam Masala and dried fenugreek leaves and mix well. Stir in the paneer and cream, mix well. Leave the curry to simmer for 3–4 minutes. Check the seasoning. Finish with the lemon juice and serve hot, with naan or roti.

PUNJABI RAJMA RASILA

This is one of my favourite dishes, a delicious and flavourful recipe made with kidney beans. A lot of beans and legumes are eaten in India, as they are the main source of protein and fibre. I like to eat rajma with plain boiled rice, onion and lime wedges.

500g (1lb 1½oz) fresh rajma (kidney beans), or 2 x 400g (14oz) tins of kidney beans
3 tablespoons ghee or cooking oil
½ teaspoon cumin seeds
1 small bay leaf or tej patta (see page 206)
250g (9oz) onions, chopped
1½ teaspoons Ginger/Garlic Paste (see page 18)
¼ teaspoon ground turmeric
½ teaspoon Kashmiri chilli powder
1 teaspoon red chilli powder
1 teaspoon Garam Masala (see page 16)
½ teaspoon amchur (dried mango powder)
1 teaspoon ground coriander
100g (3½oz) tomatoes, puréed
1 teaspoon ginger julienne
2 fresh tomatoes, diced
2 green chillies, slit in half
1 teaspoon dried fenugreek leaves
2 tablespoons chopped coriander leaves
salt

If using fresh kidney beans, rinse them, then soak them for 8 hours in lots of water. Discard the water and rinse them well. Put them into a pan, pour over 500ml (1 pint) water and cook them until they are soft but not mushy about 40–45 minutes.

Alternatively, you can use a pressure cooker. If done correctly, the rajma should be soft when you bite into it. It should not be al dente or even slightly hard. If using tinned beans, drain them and rinse them well in cold water.

Heat the ghee or oil in a pan on a medium heat and sauté the cumin seeds and bay leaf until they sizzle. Add the onions and cook until they start to turn golden brown. Stir in the Ginger/Garlic Paste and cook for a few minutes until a nice aroma starts to be released.

Add all the ground spices and a pinch of salt and sauté until the oil begins to separate. Stir in the tomatoes and cook until the raw aroma disappears. Add the cooked kidney beans, then pour in 125ml (4¼fl oz) water and stir. Add the ginger, diced tomatoes and green chillies. Cover and simmer on a low heat for 10–15 minutes.

Check that the rajma are completely cooked – when you mash the beans they must be soft. Sprinkle over the dried fenugreek leaves and stir. Scatter over the coriander to serve.

PANEER BHURJI

This is a popular northern Indian dish made with grated
or crumbled paneer, mixed peppers and ground spices. It is
eaten with chapatis, parathas, pooris or as a side dish.

50ml (1¾fl oz) rapeseed oil
1 teaspoon cumin seeds
100g (3½oz) onions, chopped
1 teaspoon chopped ginger
1 teaspoon chopped garlic
1 teaspoon ground turmeric
½ teaspoon red chilli powder
1 teaspoon ground coriander
½ teaspoon Garam Masala (see page 16)
100g (3½oz) mixed sweet peppers, diced
2 tablespoons chopped tomato
250g (9oz) paneer, grated
½ tablespoon dried fenugreek leaves
1 tablespoon chopped coriander leaves
1 tablespoon ginger julienne
salt

Heat the oil in a pan on a medium heat and
add the cumin seeds. Once they begin to
crackle, add the onions and cook until they
are light brown in colour about 8 minutes.
Add the ginger and garlic and cook until the
raw aroma disappears.

Add the ground spices, peppers and
tomatoes and cook for another 4–5 minutes.

Add the grated paneer and the dried
fenugreek leaves and mix well, then check
the seasoning, scatter over the chopped
coriander and ginger julienne and serve.

NOTE

This can also be used as a
stuffing in kathi rolls (see page
206), or in sandwiches.

TADKA DAL

This is one of the most popular Indian lentil dishes. It's commonly served in restaurants in the UK, and it's my personal favourite. I make it at least once a week at home or in the restaurant. My mother cooks toor dal (yellow split peas) a few times a week back home in India, and tempers it with ghee, cumin and garlic.

250g (9oz) toor dal (yellow split peas)
½ teaspoon ground turmeric
2–3 tablespoons ghee or cooking oil
1 teaspoon cumin seeds
2–3 dried red chillies
100g (3½oz) onions, finely chopped
4–6 garlic cloves, chopped
1 tablespoon chopped ginger
½ teaspoon red chilli powder
a pinch of asafoetida
2 green chillies, slit down one side
    or chopped
100g (3½oz) tomatoes, finely chopped
½ teaspoon Garam Masala (see page 16)
1 teaspoon lemon or lime juice (optional)
2 tablespoons chopped coriander leaves
salt

Rinse the lentils in water a couple of times. Put them into a pan with plenty of water, add a pinch each of turmeric and salt, and cook on a medium heat until the lentils are soft about 30–35 minutes. Alternatively, use a pressure cooker.

Heat the ghee or oil in a frying pan. Add the cumin seeds and dried chillies and let them cook until they begin to crackle, then add the onions and cook until they are light brown. Add the garlic and ginger and continue to cook until the raw aroma disappears.

Add the ground spices, asafoetida and green chillies and cook for few minutes. Add the tomatoes and cook until they soften and you see the oil starting to separate.

Add the cooked dal and stir, then leave on a low heat to simmer for 4–5 minutes, or until smooth and slightly thickened. Tadka dal usually has a medium to thick consistency, so adjust the amount of water you need.

Finish with the Garam Masala and lemon or lime juice (if using), and sprinkle with chopped coriander leaves.

Serve hot, with steamed basmati rice or chapatis.

PALUNGO KO SAAG

This is a wonderfully healthy and quick dish from Nepali cuisine. Palungo means fresh garden greens and spinach in the Nepali language. Saag is basically a simple stir-fry made with fresh greens and you can replace the spinach with kale or mustard leaves and serve with lentils.

500g (1lb 1½oz) baby spinach leaves
30ml (1fl oz) mustard oil
½ teaspoon cumin seeds
½ teaspoon ajwain (carom seeds)
2–3 red chillies
3–4 garlic cloves, sliced
1 tablespoon chopped garlic
125g (4½oz) onions, chopped
¼ teaspoon ground turmeric
100g (3½oz) tomatoes, chopped
¼ teaspoon ground cinnamon
½ teaspoon Garam Masala (see page 16)
salt

Wash the spinach leaves under running cold water and drain in a colander. Once completely drained, chop the spinach and put to one side.

Heat the oil in a pan. When smoking hot, lower the heat and add the cumin seeds, ajwain and red chillies. Once the seeds start crackling, add the sliced and garlic along with the chopped onions and sauté for couple of minutes. When the onions start to turn golden brown, add the turmeric and a pinch of salt, give a good stir, then add the tomatoes and cook for 3 minutes.

Add the spinach to the pan and mix well, then cook, uncovered, for about 7–8 minutes until the spinach is wilted and tender. Check the seasoning, then add the cinnamon and Garam Masala and mix well before serving.

PINDI CHANA

This dish is named after the town where it originated – Rawalpindi in Pakistan – in the days before the India-Pakistan partition. It's easy to cook and, unusually, does not contain any onion or garlic.

TO BE BOILED

300g (10½oz) chickpeas
2 tea bags
1 teaspoon amla pieces (see page 206)
2 black cardamoms
2–3 green cardamoms
2–3 cloves
2.5cm (1in) piece of cinnamon stick
1 bay leaf
1 teaspoon salt

TO BE DRY ROASTED

1 tablespoon pomegranate seeds
1 tablespoon cumin seeds
2 tablespoons coriander seeds
½ teaspoon ajwain (carom seeds)

TO COMPLETE THE DISH

2 tablespoons ground coriander
½ teaspoon Garam Masala (see page 16)
1 teaspoon amchur (dried mango powder)
¼ teaspoon black salt
a pinch of asafoetida
1 teaspoon crushed dried fenugreek leaves
½ teaspoon red chilli powder
2 teaspoons Kashmiri chilli powder
4 green chillies, slit down one side
    and seeds removed
2 tablespoons ginger julienne
50ml (1¾fl oz) rapeseed oil
1 tablespoon finely chopped
    coriander leaves
1–2 lemon wedges
salt

Rinse the chickpeas and put them into a pan with the rest of the boiling ingredients. Bring to the boil, then lower the heat and simmer for 8–10 minutes. The tea bags and amla will turn the chickpeas a dark brown colour. Once this happens, turn off the heat and drain the chickpeas, reserving the liquid. Set aside.

Meanwhile, put the roasting ingredients into a pan and dry roast on a low heat. Keep stirring constantly to make sure the spices do not burn. Otherwise the chana will taste bitter. When the spices have cooled, grind them to a fine powder.

Put the boiled chickpeas into a large bowl along with 2 tablespoons of the dry roasted mixture, the ground coriander, Garam Masala, dried mango powder, black salt, asafoetida, fenugreek leaves and both chilli powders. Mix well to coat every chickpea with the spice mixture. Add the slit chillies and two-thirds of the ginger julienne.

Heat the oil in a kadai or pan and add the chickpea mixture. Gradually add the reserved cooking liquid until you get the desired consistency. Mix well. Leave to simmer on a low heat until the oil separates.

Dish up the pindi chana in a serving bowl, garnished with coriander, the remaining ginger julienne and lemon wedges.

Roti & Chawal

RICE AND BREADS

BHUTEKO BHAT
(NEPALESE FRIED RICE)

Bhuteko bhat is a very quick recipe to which you can also add seasonal vegetables. Every region has a different style of fried rice dish – bhuteko bhat is generally eaten with pickles and can be served with a curry, but fried rice is very rarely served with dal.

1 tablespoon ghee
a pinch of asafoetida
5g cumin seeds
2–3 dried red chillies
2 garlic cloves, chopped
2 onions, thinly sliced
250g (9oz) cooked rice
¼ teaspoon ground cinnamon
2 tablespoons chopped spring onions
1 tablespoon Fried Onions (see page 21)
salt

Heat the ghee in a heavy-based pan, then add the asafoetida and cumin seeds followed by the red chillies.

Add the garlic and onions and cook for a few minutes until golden brown. Add the rice, mix well, then stir in the cinnamon, spring onions and fried onions and season with salt. Serve hot.

NOTE

Spring onions should always be included in this recipe, but you can also add seasonal vegetables. For example, peas, carrots, peppers, baby corn, shredded broccoli and cauliflower.

JACKFRUIT BIRYANI

Biryani is popular across India, as well as in the rest of the world, and every region has its own style and ingredients. Two Indian styles of biryani are very famous: Hyderabadi and Lucknowi. Traditional biryani is a combination of basmati rice, mutton, chicken and vegetables. Most people make it with meat, but I've tried a different style of biryani here, using jackfruit. I prefer this to a meat biryani, because of its texture, flavours and spices. *Pictured overleaf.*

200g (7oz) basmati rice

8 whole green cardamoms

4 black cardamoms

8 cloves

50g (1¾oz) ghee, plus a little for greasing and drizzling

50ml (1¾fl oz) rapeseed oil, plus extra for deep-frying

250g (9oz) tinned jackfruit

1 teaspoon black cumin seeds (shahi jeera)

2.5cm (1in) piece of cinnamon stick

1 bay leaf

½ teaspoon whole black peppercorns

100g (3½oz) onions, finely sliced

1 tablespoon Ginger/Garlic Paste `(see page 18)

2 green chillies, slit down one side

1 teaspoon Garam Masala (see page 16), plus a little extra to sprinkle

½ teaspoon Kashmiri chilli powder

¼ teaspoon ground turmeric

1 tablespoon ground coriander

60g (2oz) yoghurt

1 tablespoon rose water

50g (1¾oz) Fried Onions (see page 21)

2 tablespoons chopped coriander leaves

2 tablespoons chopped mint leaves

2 tablespoons kewra water (see page 206)

1 tablespoon coarse black pepper

a generous pinch of saffron strands, soaked in 30ml (1fl oz) warm milk

salt

raita, to serve

Soak the rice in 750ml (1 pint 9fl oz) water for 30 minutes, then drain in a colander.

Put a large pan of water on a medium heat and add a pinch of salt and half the green cardamoms, black cardamoms and cloves. Bring to the boil and add the rice, giving it a stir with a spoon. Let it cook uncovered until it's almost ready, then remove the pan from the heat and drain the rice in a colander. Stir the ghee into the drained rice to increase the flavour, then set aside.

Heat the oil for deep-frying to 170°C/340°F in a large pan. Wash the pieces of jackfruit under running water. Put them in a colander to drain off the excess water, then deep-fry them and set aside.

Heat the oil in a pan on a medium heat. Add the black cumin seeds, cinnamon stick, bay leaf, peppercorns and the remaining cardamoms and cloves. Stir and let the spices sizzle for few seconds. Add the onions and cook until they start to turn golden brown. Add the Ginger/Garlic Paste and the green chillies and cook for 2 minutes, until the raw aroma disappears.

Add the pieces of fried jackfruit, give them a stir, then add the Garam Masala, Kashmiri chilli powder, turmeric, ground coriander and a pinch of salt and cook

for 2–3 minutes. Add 50ml (1¾fl oz) water and mix well, then remove the pan from the heat and stir in the yoghurt. Put the pan back on the heat and cook for around 8–10 minutes. There shouldn't be much liquid left. Remove from the heat.

Grease a heavy-based pan with ghee. Add half the rice in a layer, sprinkle with half the rose water, then top with half the fried onions and half the coriander and mint. Add ½ teaspoon of the kewra water. Spoon the jackfruit mixture on top, and add the rest of the rice in a layer on top of the jackfruit. Top with the remaining fried onion, coriander and mint and scatter over the coarse black pepper. Sprinkle over the saffron milk and the remaining rose water.

Finally drizzle 1 teaspoon of ghee on top and sprinkle over some Garam Masala. Cover the pan tightly, first with foil, then with a well-fitting lid. Heat a flat pan on a medium heat. Once hot, reduce the heat to its lowest. Place your biryani pan on top of the flat pan and let it cook for 10–15 minutes on the lowest heat.

Remove from the heat and set aside for 8–10 minutes, then remove the lid and foil and serve with raita.

MISSI ROTI

This flatbread made with chickpea flour is a Punjabi speciality and is usually made during the winter on a tandoor or a griddle. It goes well with Indian curries. It's also eaten at breakfast time, with pickles and yoghurt, and a good gluten-free option.

100g (3½oz) whole wheat flour, plus extra for dusting
240g (8½oz) besan (gram flour), plus extra for dusting
1 teaspoon salt
1 teaspoon ajwain (carom seeds)
50g (1¾oz) onions, finely chopped
1–2 green chillies, finely chopped
1 tablespoon dried fenugreek leaves
a pinch of asafoetida
3 teaspoons rapeseed or vegetable oil, plus extra for the dough

Put the whole wheat flour, gram flour, salt and ajwain into a mixing bowl. Add the remaining ingredients and mix very well. Add 125ml (4¼fl oz) water and begin to mix and knead to a smooth, soft dough, adding more water as required – the amount will depend on the quality of the flour.

Leave the dough to rest for 10 minutes, then divide it into equal-sized balls. Dust with flour and roll out to a circle of about 12–15cm (5–6in), dusting with more flour if needed.

Place the roti on a hot tawa or griddle. When the base is partially cooked after about 2–3 minutes, flip the roti over and spread some oil on the cooked side. When the second side is cooked and brown spots start to be seen, flip again. Flip once or twice more, so that the roti is evenly cooked.

Serve hot or warm, with dal, a sabzi or a pickle.

MAKKI KI ROTI

This popular Punjabi flatbread is made from maize flour and is generally served with sarson ka saag (mustard leaf), a vegetable that's very widely used during the winter time. Makki is a Punjabi word for maize (corn), and a yellow flour made from maize is the base ingredient for this recipe. My mother used to make this roti in the traditional way, flattening a dough ball into a round shape by repeatedly pressing it in between her palms with a thumping motion, then cooking it on a hot tawa.

240g (8½oz) maize flour (makki ka atta), plus extra for rolling
60g (2oz) besan (gram flour)
vegetable oil, for roasting
salt

Put the maize flour, gram flour and a pinch of salt into a mixing bowl and stir them together with a spoon. Add 250ml (8½fl oz) warm water and mix well, then set aside for 10 minutes.

Place the dough on a floured board and knead to a smooth yet firm dough. If it looks dry, add more warm water. If it looks sticky, add a few more tablespoons of maize flour. Divide the mixture into equal-sized balls and use a rolling pin to flatten each one into a rough circle.

You can also make makki roti by patting out the dough. Sprinkle some maize flour all over the dough ball and also on the board. Now, with your fingers, gently press and pat the dough, moving it clockwise as you press, and adding flour as required, until you get a neat makki roti. Do not make them too thin.

Spread some oil on a hot tawa or griddle. Gently add the roti to the hot surface – if there are any cracks in the roti, gently pat them with a few drops of water. When one side starts to get a bit brown, flip the roti with the help of a spatula. When the other side is browned, flip again. Flip a couple more times, until the roti is well browned and cooked on both sides. Serve hot.

TIP

The traditional method my mother would use to roll the dough needs practice, so I recommend that you use a rolling pin here.

CHAPATI

Chapati is a type of Indian flatbread that is very popular throughout India. It is a staple dish and is made from really simple ingredients – wheat flour, salt and water. Serve this with dal or a veggie dish.

250g (9oz) whole wheat
    or multigrain flour
a pinch of salt
1 tablespoon rapeseed oil

Put the flour, salt and oil into a bowl and mix well, then add 75ml (2½fl oz) warm water and mix well with your hands, adding more water (up to 150ml/5fl oz in total) until you have a soft dough. The mixture should be neither too dry or nor too wet.

Divide the dough into 6 equal pieces and roll out each one to a thickness of 2–3mm.

Heat a pan or tawa (griddle) until hot, then slide the rolled chapati onto the hot surface and cook for 1–2 minutes, until the roti starts to puff up. Flip the roti over and cook on the other side for 1 minute.

NOTE

If you would like to make this a more nutritious addition to your meal, use multigrain flour.

ZARDA
(SWEET PULAO)

This dish is very popular in northern India. It's made with basmati rice, saffron and jaggery. It is typically served as a dessert after a meal, although it can also be served during the meal at special occasions and celebrations or as here, as a side. I learned this recipe from my mum, who always makes it with jaggery. Usually in India people use sugar, but according to my mum, jaggery works really well with cloves in terms of flavour and sweetness. She always makes this during winter time. The name of this dish has its origins in Persian, the word 'zard' meaning a bright yellow colour.

120g (4oz) basmati rice
60g (2oz) ghee
8 cashews
5 almonds, chopped
2 teaspoons raisins
2 teaspoons desiccated coconut
2 green cardamoms
4 cloves
¼ teaspoon saffron
100g (3½oz) jaggery, grated

Soak the rice in plenty of water for 30 minutes, then drain and set aside.

Heat half the ghee in a large kadai or pan and add the cashews, almonds, raisins and coconut. Cook on a low heat until the nuts are golden brown, then remove from the pan and set aside.

Add the remaining ghee to the pan, along with the cardamoms and cloves. Add 180ml (6fl oz) water and the saffron. Add the soaked basmati rice and mix well, then cover the pan and cook on a medium heat for 10 minutes.

After 10 minutes, stir gently and check – the rice should be half cooked by now. Add the grated jaggery and the roasted dried nuts and fruits, reserving a few to garnish. Stir, making sure the jaggery has dissolved, then cover and simmer for 5 minutes, stirring regularly to prevent it burning. Continue to cook until the rice is cooked completely, but do not overcook or it will turn mushy.

Serve hot, garnished with the reserved chopped nuts and fruits.

BUTTER NAAN

A naan is a soft, pillowy, folded and triangular-shaped Indian-style flatbread traditionally made in a tandoor. It's widely available in supermarkets, but it is even tastier made from scratch. This goes really well with any Indian food. I especially like to serve butter naan with black lentils. *Pictured overleaf.*

1kg (2lb) refined white flour or self-raising flour, plus extra for dusting
1 teaspoon baking powder
a pinch of salt
2 teaspoons sugar
1 egg
240ml (8fl oz) milk
1 tablespoon rapeseed oil
2 teaspoons butter

Sift the flour with the baking powder and salt. Add the sugar, egg and milk and knead well until you have a medium soft dough, adding a little water if you need it. Rub the dough with a little oil and keep it under a damp cloth for 1 hour.

Divide the dough into 8 equal-sized balls. Rub each one with a little oil, then press first the sides, then the centre of each dough ball to give it a round flat shape. Pat it out to about 15cm (6in) in diameter. Brush with oil and dust with flour, then fold it in half to make a semicircle. Rub with oil and dust with flour again, then fold in half.

Roll out with a rolling pin or press with your fingertips, making sure the edges are properly thinned out. Stretch it on one side to make a triangular shape.

Cook the naan in a preheated oven at 180°C/350°F/gas mark 4 for 4–5 minutes, or on a hot tawa or griddle, until crisp and lightly browned on both sides.

Serve hot, topped with the butter.

VEG TEHRI
(SEASONAL GREENS WITH RICE)

Veg tehri is an aromatic, spiced rice and vegetable dish that's popular in northern India. Rice and vegetables are cooked together along with spices – it's easy to make and should be slightly moist.

300g (10½oz) basmati rice
50ml (1¾fl oz) rapeseed oil
1 tablespoon cumin seeds
1 bay leaf
4 green cardamoms
2 black cardamoms
100g (3½oz) onions, sliced
1 tablespoon Ginger/Garlic Paste
  (see page 18)
100g (3½oz) potatoes, diced
100g (3½oz) carrots, diced
3 green chillies, slit down one side
50g (1¾oz) French beans, cut into batons
100g (3½oz) green peas, fresh or frozen
100g (3½oz) cauliflower florets
1 teaspoon red chilli powder
1 tablespoon ground coriander
½ teaspoon ground turmeric
150g (5oz) tomatoes, chopped
1 tablespoons chopped mint leaves
3 tablespoons chopped coriander leaves
salt
raita or pickle, to serve

Rinse the rice in cold water until the water runs clear. Soak the rice in plenty of water for 30 minutes, then drain and set aside.

Heat the oil to 170°C/340°F in a deep, heavy-based pan. Add the cumin seeds, bay leaf, green and black cardamoms and sauté until the spices crackle and become fragrant. Add the onions and cook on a low heat with a pinch of salt until they start to turn golden brown. Add the Ginger/Garlic Paste and cook for a few seconds until the raw aroma disappears.

Add the potatoes and carrots to the pan and cook for 4–5 minutes on a low heat. Add the green chillies, French beans, peas and cauliflower and stir well. Add the red chilli powder, ground coriander, turmeric and a pinch of salt and mix well, then add the tomatoes and cook for a minute or two.

Add the rice, stir very well and cook for a minute. Add 750ml (1 pint 9fl oz) water and the chopped mint and coriander leaves, then cover the pan with a tight lid and cook on a low heat for about 15–20 minutes, until all the water has been absorbed and the rice grains are fluffy and soft.

Remove from the heat and leave to stand for 5 minutes before removing the lid. Then gently fluff up the rice and serve with a raita or pickle.

CHICKPEA AND MUSHROOM BIRYANI

Biryani is very popular. I am always trying out new versions with
different ingredients and vegetables. Many people enjoy vegetable
biryani, so I've made a version with chickpeas and mushrooms.
But feel free to use your own selection here.
Pictured overleaf.

FOR THE CHICKPEAS AND MUSHROOMS

200g (7oz) tinned chickpeas
2–3 tablespoons rapeseed oil
1 teaspoon black cumin seeds (shahi jeera)
2–3 green cardamoms
1 black cardamom
4cm (1½in) cinnamon stick
1 bay leaf
2–3 cloves
160g (5½oz) onions, finely sliced
200g (7oz) portobello mushrooms,
    cut into small dice
1 tablespoon Ginger/Garlic Paste
    (see page 18)
2–3 green chillies, slit down one side
100g (3½oz) tomatoes, chopped
100g (3½oz) yoghurt
½ teaspoon ground turmeric
½ teaspoon red chilli powder
1 tablespoon ground coriander
salt

FOR THE RICE

200g (7oz) basmati rice
2–3 green cardamoms
1 black cardamom
2–4cm (1–1½in) piece of cinnamon stick
2–3 blades of mace
1 bay leaf
3 cloves

TO ASSEMBLE THE BIRYANI

1 tablespoon ghee
2 tablespoons chopped mint leaves
2 tablespoons chopped coriander leaves
2 tablespoons ginger julienne
1 teaspoon coarse black pepper
a pinch of saffron strands, soaked in
    30ml (1fl oz) warm milk
2 tablespoons rose water
1 teaspoon Garam Masala (see page 16)
¼ teaspoon ground green cardamom
2 tablespoons lime juice

Rinse the chickpeas under cold running
water and set aside. Soak the basmati rice
in plenty of water for 30 minutes, then drain
and set aside.

To cook the rice, heat 750ml (1 pint 9fl oz)
water in a pan. When the water is hot, add
the green cardamoms, black cardamom,
cinnamon stick, mace, bay leaf, cloves and
a pinch of salt. Bring the water to a rolling
boil on a high heat and add the strained rice.
Cook on a high heat until the rice is nearly
cooked and has a slight bite, then switch
off the heat. Immediately drain the rice and
set aside.

CONTINUED OVERLEAF

While the rice is soaking and cooking, you can prepare the chickpeas and mushrooms. Heat 2 tablespoons of oil and add the black cumin seeds, green cardamoms, black cardamom, cinnamon stick, bay leaf and cloves. Sauté the spices for a few seconds, until they start to crackle, then add the onions and stir well. Sauté the onions on a medium heat until they become golden, then turn off the heat and transfer the fried onions to a plate. Set aside.

Heat a tablespoon of oil in a second pan and cook the mushrooms with a little salt until they start to turn golden brown – you will need to do this in at least two batches. Remove from the pan and set aside.

Add the Ginger/Garlic Paste and green chillies to the pan and cook until the raw aroma disappears. Add the tomatoes and cook for a minute. Add the turmeric, red chilli powder, ground coriander and a pinch of salt and stir well. Add the mushrooms and drained chickpeas to the pan and mix everything well. Add the yoghurt and about 100ml (3½fl oz) water and cook on a medium heat for another 10–12 minutes. Check the seasoning.

To assemble the biryani, grease a heavy-based pan with ghee. Add half the rice, in one layer, and top with half the fried onions, half the coriander and half the mint. Sprinkle over ½ teaspoon of the rose water and spoon the chickpea and mushroom mixture on top. Add the rest of the rice in a layer, and top with the rest of the fried onions. Scatter over the coarse black pepper, ginger julienne and the rest of the coriander and mint. Drizzle over the saffron milk and the remaining rose water. Finally, drizzle over 1 teaspoon ghee and sprinkle over the Garam Masala, ground green cardamom and lime juice.

Cover the pan tightly, first with foil, then with a well-fitting lid. Heat a flat pan on a medium heat. Once hot, reduce the heat to its lowest. Place your biryani pan on top of the flat pan and let it cook for 10–15 minutes on the lowest heat. Remove from the heat and set it aside, then remove the lid and foil and serve with cucumber raita.

CHUR CHUR PARATHA

This is one of my favourite parathas, and I used to have it at least 3 or 4 times a week when I was a kid. The ones my mum makes are so delicious, always served with a knob of butter. You can eat them on their own – you don't need any curry.

400g (14oz) whole wheat or multigrain
   flour, plus extra for dusting
1 tsp ajwain (carom seeds)
5 teaspoons rapeseed oil
1 tablespoon butter
salt

Put the flour, ajwain and a pinch of salt into a mixing bowl and knead the flour with as much water as you need (about 250ml/8½fl oz) to make a soft dough. Remember to add the water gradually, and to keep stirring the flour with your hands. This should take about 5–7 minutes.

When you finish kneading, add 2 teaspoons of the oil and knead again to get a soft texture. Cover with a damp cloth and leave for at least 10 minutes. Divide the dough into equal-sized balls and roll each one into a nice round roti. Brush with oil, then fold it in half so you have a semicircle.

Brush with oil and fold again, so you have a triangular shape. Dip it into some flour and roll out on each side, making sure the edges are properly thinned out.

Heat the tawa and when hot, add the paratha. After about 30 seconds, flip it over. Brush the top side of the paratha with oil and turn it over, continuing the same way for the other side. The parathas should have brown spots on both sides.

Before serving, add a knob of butter.

Achar & Chutney

PICKLES AND DIPS

COCONUT CHUTNEY

Coconut chutney is a southern Indian chutney and a perfect accompaniment to dosa and idli (see page 32). This is also wonderful served with main course or curry.

2 tablespoons fried gram
(or 1½ tablespoons chana dal/split chickpeas plus ½ tablespoon urad dal/split black gram)
200g (7oz) chopped
or grated coconut
50g (1¾oz) coriander leaves,
including tender stalks
1 tablespoon ginger, chopped
1–2 green chillies
salt

FOR THE TEMPERING

1 teaspoon rapeseed oil
1 teaspoon mustard seeds
1 dried red chilli, broken up
a sprig of curry leaves
a pinch of asafoetida (optional)

Dry roast the dals in a pan on a medium heat until golden and aromatic, then turn off the heat and leave to cool. Put them in a food processor or blender with the coconut, coriander, ginger, green chillies and a pinch of salt and blend to a smooth, thick chutney, adding a little water if needed.

For the tempering, heat the oil in a small pan and add the mustard seeds and red chilli. When the seeds start to crackle, add the curry leaves and the asafoetida, if using. Once the curry leaves turn crisp, pour the contents of the pan over the chutney. Give it a stir and serve.

CAULIFLOWER PICKLE

Pickles are very popular in Indian cuisine as they go so well with lentils, paratha and pulao dishes. Every region has their own style. You can buy pickles in most shops, but I think making your own is well worth the effort.

500g (1lb 1½oz) small cauliflower florets
100ml (3½fl oz) mustard oil
1 tablespoon panch phoron (pickling spices
　– you can buy this ready-made)
½ teaspoon asafoetida
1 teaspoon ground turmeric
1 teaspoon red chilli powder
1 tablespoon ground coriander
40g (1½oz) jaggery (see page 176) or
　palm sugar
60g (2oz) granulated sugar
50ml (1¾fl oz) white wine vinegar
salt

Blanch the cauliflower florets in salted water for 3–4 minutes, then drain and put into iced water.

Heat the mustard oil in a pan on a medium heat and add the panch phoron. Once they begin to crackle, add the ground spices, jaggery, sugar and vinegar. Cook on a low heat until the sugar and jaggery have dissolved completely.

Pour the mixture over the cooled cauliflower. Transfer to an airtight jar and store in the fridge for 3–4 weeks.

RAW MANGO CHUTNEY
(AAM KI LAUNJI)

This is my mum's recipe that she always makes during the summer season in India, when raw mangoes are widely available. She also makes a raw mango drink, which is very popular – everyone loves to drink it during the summer months. *Pictured on page 174.*

250g (9oz) raw green mangoes,
   peeled and grated
2 tablespoons rapeseed oil
½ teaspoon onion seeds
½ teaspoon ground turmeric
½ teaspoon red chilli powder
2 tablespoons white vinegar
75g (2½oz) jaggery, grated (see page 176)
50g (1¾oz) caster sugar
salt

Wash and peel the mangoes, then grate and set aside.

Heat the oil in a pan on a medium heat. Add the onion seeds and give them a quick stir, then add the turmeric, red chilli powder and a pinch of salt and stir again. Add the grated raw mango and the vinegar and sauté everything for 1 minute. Lower the temperature and let the mango cook for 3–4 minutes.

Add the grated jaggery and sugar and cook on a low heat for 10–15 minutes, adding a little water if needed and stirring regularly.

Check the seasoning – the chutney should be sweet, spicy and a little sour in taste. Give it a quick stir and turn off the heat. Transfer to a clean, dry jar or a serving dish.

GREEN MINT CHUTNEY

This is a versatile green chutney that goes very well with Indian snacks. I like to serve it with tadka dal (see page 139) and plain rice. It's usually made with a smaller amount of mint than coriander, but in this recipe I use equal quantities of each. You can add onion as well, if you like.

Makes 120g (4oz)

50g (1¾oz) mint leaves
50g (1¾oz) coriander leaves
2 teaspoons fresh ginger, peeled and roughly chopped
2 green chillies, roughly chopped
1 tablespoon natural yoghurt (or soya yoghurt, if preferred)
1 tablespoon lime juice
¼ teaspoon black salt

Put everything into a food processor or blender and blend to a fine paste. Adjust the seasoning to taste.

TOMATO CHUTNEY

This is so simple and versatile. It is especially delicious with idli and dosas.

Makes 500g (1lb 1½oz)

2 tablespoons rapeseed oil
1 tablespoon chana dal (split chickpeas)
3–4 large garlic cloves
1 tablespoon ginger, peeled and chopped
100g (3½oz) onions, chopped
2–3 dried red Kashmiri chillies
350g (12¼oz) tomatoes, roughly chopped
½ teaspoon salt
½ teaspoon Kashmiri chilli powder

FOR THE TADKA

1 teaspoon oil (use your oil of choice)
¼ teaspoon mustard seeds
a pinch of asafoetida
6–7 curry leaves

Heat the oil in a pan on a medium heat. Cook the chana dal for 2–3 minutes, or until golden in colour. Add the garlic, ginger, onions and dried red chillies, increasing the amount of chillies according to your taste.

Cook for 3–4 minutes until the onions are soft. Stir in the tomatoes and salt. Cook on a medium heat for about 6–7 minutes until the tomatoes are soft and mushy.

Let the mixture cool a little, then transfer it to a food processor or blender. Add the chilli powder and blitz to a smooth paste.

For the tadka, heat the oil in a small pan on a medium heat. Add the mustard seeds and once they start to crackle, add the asafoetida and the curry leaves and cook for a minute until crisp.

Pour the tadka on top of the chutney.

MIXED WILD BERRY CHUTNEY

Chutneys are very popular as they go well with both sweet and savoury dishes, especially snacks and poppadums. I am always experimenting, and when I tried making this wild berry chutney with Indian spices, I was so pleased with how well it worked. *Pictured overleaf.*

Makes 650g (1lb 7oz)

500g (1lb 1½oz) frozen wild berries
2 tablespoons chopped ginger
1 green chilli, chopped
½ teaspoon red chilli powder
2 star anise
½ teaspoon salt
1½ teaspoons black salt
100g (3½oz) caster sugar
2 tablespoons white vinegar

Heat a pan and add all the ingredients. Cook on a low heat, stirring, for a few minutes, until the berries are soft.

Mash the mixture and allow the chutney to cool.

CORIANDER AND MINT CHUTNEY

Simple, quick and flavourful, coriander and mint chutney is one of the best accompaniments to Indian food. I enjoy it with spicy tadka dal (see page 139) and plain rice. *Pictured overleaf.*

Makes 250g (9oz)

50g (1¾oz) yoghurt
3 tablespoons fresh lemon juice
100g (3½oz) coriander, leaves and stalks
50g (1¾oz) mint leaves
2 green chillies, sliced
2 teaspoons roughly chopped ginger
2 garlic cloves, crushed
½ teaspoon salt
¼ tsp black salt

Put all the ingredients into a food processor or blender with 1 tablespoon water and blend until smooth. Taste and adjust the seasoning. Add a little more water if you need to adjust the texture.

Serve with your starters or main course.

TAMARIND CHUTNEY

Sweet, spicy and tangy, this is also known as imli ki chutney. It's made with tamarind, jaggery and spices, and is a staple chutney used in India for all street food and chaats (snacks). The best thing about this is that it will go with all hot and cold fried snacks.

100g (3½oz) seedless tamarind
1 tablespoon ground coriander
½ teaspoon ground ginger
1 teaspoon red chilli powder
50ml (1¾fl oz) rapeseed oil
50g (1¾oz) jaggery (see below)
50g (1¾oz) caster sugar
1 teaspoon salt
1 tablespoon ginger, chopped

Put the tamarind, ground coriander, ground ginger and red chilli powder into a small bowl and add 300ml (10fl oz) water. Leave to soak for at least 4–5 hours or preferably overnight.

Heat the oil in a pan. Add the soaked tamarind mixture and cook over a medium heat for 20–25 minutes, stirring regularly. Once the mixture starts to boil, add the jaggery, sugar and salt and cook for a further 4–5 minutes until the mixture has thickened. Strain through a fine sieve, then check the consistency and seasoning. Transfer to another pan and cook for 4–5 minutes, then turn off the heat, stir in the chopped ginger and leave to cool.

When cooled, decant into an airtight jar or container and store in the fridge.

NOTE

Jaggery is a very rich unrefined sugar that is cooked down and reduced and sold as blocks.

MOOLI PICKLE

Pickles are very popular in Indian cuisine and go well with lentils, paratha and pulao dishes. My mother always makes pickles at home, and she has shared a lot of her recipes with me. I always follow her instructions very carefully while making pickle! She used to make a spicy turnip pickle, which was the inspiration for this version with radish. This is very easy to make and store.

300g (10½oz) radishes or mooli, peeled and cut into medium-thick slices
1½ teaspoons salt
½ teaspoon ground turmeric
2 tablespoons split mustard seeds
200ml (7fl oz) mustard oil
2 tablespoons red chilli powder
1½ tablespoons fennel seeds, crushed
2 tablespoons white vinegar

Put the radish or mooli in a mixing bowl with the salt, turmeric and mustard seeds. Mix well, then cover and set aside for 8 hours or overnight.

Heat the mustard oil in a pan. Once hot, turn off the heat and let it cool to room temperature. Pour it over the radishes, add the chilli powder, fennel seeds and vinegar and mix well.

Cover with a muslin cloth and leave the pickle to mature for at least 3–4 days at room temperature. Once ready, store it in the fridge.

AVOCADO CHUTNEY

**This avocado chutney is easy, quick, healthy and nutritious.
Spread it on toast or serve it with parathas or snacks.**

2 avocados
75g (2½oz) coriander leaves,
    roughly chopped
50g (1¾oz) mint leaves, roughly chopped
25g (1oz) ginger, roughly chopped
6 garlic cloves, chopped (optional)
4–6 long green chillies, deseeded
    and cut into pieces
½ teaspoon toasted cumin seeds
1 small tomato, deseeded and chopped
3 tablespoons olive oil
1 tablespoon lime juice
salt

Wash the avocados, then cut them in half and remove the stones. Using a spoon, scoop out the pulp into a bowl and smash it with a fork.

Put the coriander, mint, ginger, garlic (if using) and green chillies in a food processor or blender and blitz coarsely. Add the blended mixture to the avocado.

Add the toasted cumin, tomato, olive oil, lime juice and salt to taste.

Mix evenly and correct the seasoning, if necessary, before serving.

Meetha

DESSERTS

POACHED PEARS

Poached pears are an ideal winter and Christmas dessert, and it's very easy to make them at home. The pears are poached in red wine or fruit juices, with spices and sugar and are usually served with flavoured glaze or ice cream.

500ml (1 pint) water
100ml (3½fl oz) maple syrup
a generous pinch of saffron
1 star anise
3–4 green cardamoms
½ teaspoon vanilla extract
1 tablespoon ginger julienne
4 small pears, peeled, halved and cored

TOPPINGS

vegan ice cream
nuts
dried fruit
a dusting of nutmeg or cinnamon

In a medium, high-sided saucepan set on a medium heat, combine the water, maple syrup, saffron, star anise, green cardamoms, vanilla and ginger. Bring the mixture to a simmer.

Place the pears in the syrup mixture and simmer for 45 minutes, or until they are tender and soft, then remove them from the heat and leave to cool. Boil the leftover syrup until it has reduced to a sticky glaze. Set aside to cool slightly. Place the poached pears in a serving bowl and pour some of the warm glaze on top of each pear. Serve with toppings of your choice.

AAMRAS POORI

Aamras poori is a very popular dessert from Maharashtra and Gujarat. During the summer, when mangoes are in season, people love this simple and delicious dessert made with fresh mango pulp and served with cocktail-size poori, a deep-fried bread.

FOR THE AAMRAS

400g (14oz) ripe Alphonso mangoes
    or mango pulp
¼ teaspoon ground ginger
½ teaspoon ground cardamom
a pinch of saffron strands, crushed
sugar, to taste
1 tablespoon chopped dried fruit
water or milk, as needed

FOR THE POORIS

200g (7oz) plain flour
2 tablespoons fine semolina (sooji)
¼ teaspoon ajwain (carom seeds)
a few strands of saffron, soaked in
    a little warm milk
1 tablespoon rapeseed oil, plus extra
    for deep-frying
salt

Peel and chop the mangoes, then blitz in a food processor or blender. Stir in the ground ginger and cardamom and the saffron strands. Add the sugar, depending on taste, and some milk or water if you would like it thinner in texture. Pour into small bowls, garnish with dried fruits and chill in the refrigerator.

To make the pooris, put the flour, fine semolina and ajwain into a bowl and add salt to taste. Add the saffron and milk to the flour mixture – the saffron will give colour and flavour to the pooris. Mix everything together very well. Add the oil, then start to add water a little at a time, to form a dough. Knead the dough really well, adding more water as required – it may appear quite firm at first, but as you continue to knead it will become slightly soft.

The semolina absorbs water while you knead, so if the dough looks sticky, don't worry. Continue to knead and the stickiness will disappear. The final dough should not be too soft. Cover the dough and leave it to rest for 30 minutes.

Now knead the dough lightly again. Divide it into small to medium pieces, shape them into balls, put them on a tray and cover. Take one of the dough balls at a time and slightly flatten it between your palms. Rub both sides with oil. Gently roll out to a small or medium disc. Make the rest of the poori the same way.

Heat the oil to 160°C/320°F in a deep frying pan or kadai. When it's hot enough, add the poori, one at a time – they will start to puff up. Once both sides are crisp and golden, about 4–6 minutes, remove them from the oil with a slotted spoon.

Serve the crispy saffron-flavoured poori with the chilled aamras.

ROSE AND CASHEW BARFI

Kaju katli, also known as kaju (cashew) barfi, is an Indian dessert made with gram flour, lentils and dried milk. Barfi is often, but not always, made by thickening milk with sugar and other ingredients. This includes wonderfully fragrant dried rose petals and rose water.

250g (9oz) cashews
1 tablespoon cornflour
60ml (2fl oz) water
125g (4½oz) caster sugar
¼ teaspoon ground cardamom
2 tablespoons dried rose petals
1 tablespoon rose water

Put the cashews and cornflour into a food processor or blender and blitz to a fine powder. Set aside.

Put the sugar and water in a saucepan on a medium heat and mix well. Bring to the boil, about 3 minutes. Continue to cook on a medium heat, stirring a few times, until the syrup reaches single thread consistency (see note below). The syrup will get bubbly while it thickens. Stir in the cardamom.

Reduce the heat to low, then stir in half the ground cashews. Keep adding the cashews, a few tablespoons at a time, until the mixture gets thick. Add the dried rose petals and rose water, mix well and cook for another 3–4 minutes. The mixture will be somewhere between a thick batter and a soft dough.

Transfer the hot mixture to a piece of baking parchment or a greased flat plate or pan. Carefully pat it down, using a spatula, into a 5mm (¼in) thick rectangle. If the mixture is too sticky or hot, let it cool for a minute before patting it down. You can also roll it between two pieces of baking parchment. Before shaping, you can knead the mixture a bit to make it smoother.

Using a knife, score the rectangle into squares. Leave to cool completely before separating into pieces. Store in an airtight container for a few days in a cool place, or for several weeks in the fridge.

SINGLE THREAD CONSISTENCY

Making sure the syrup is not too hot, take a drop of syrup carefully between one finger and thumb or between two spoons. When you separate your finger and thumb/spoons, the syrup should form a single thread at least 1cm (½in) long before breaking.

MALPUA

Malpuas are sweet pancakes fried in ghee and dipped in sugar syrup. They are a festive delight, and are traditionally made during festivals such as Holi and Diwali. They are very popular in Uttar Pradesh, Rajasthan, Bihar, West Bengal, Orissa and Maharashtra, and each region has a different version. *Pictured overleaf.*

FOR THE SUGAR SYRUP

250g (9oz) caster sugar
180ml (6fl oz) water
4 green cardamoms
a few saffron strands
1 teaspoon lemon juice

FOR THE MALPUAS

150g (5oz) plain flour
50g (1¾oz) milk powder
1 teaspoon fennel seeds
1 tablespoon caster sugar
½ teaspoon green cardamom powder
a pinch of baking powder
350ml (12fl oz) water
300ml (10fl oz) rapeseed oil or ghee, for frying
2 tablespoons chopped mixed nuts (almonds, pistachios, cashews)

To make the sugar syrup, put the sugar and water into a pan on a medium heat. Add the cardamom pods and saffron strands. Once the sugar has dissolved, boil the syrup until it becomes sticky (single thread consistency, see note opposite). Add the lemon juice and stir well (the lemon juice helps to prevent the syrup crystallising).

To make the batter for the malpuas, put the flour and milk powder into a large bowl. Add the fennel seeds, sugar, cardamom powder and baking powder and mix well. Start slowly adding the water, whisking to form a smooth batter with no lumps. It should be a thick batter of pouring consistency. Let it rest for 10–15 minutes.

Heat the oil or ghee in a wide pan on a medium heat. Pour a small ladle of batter into the hot oil – it will form a round shape on its own, you don't need to shape it. Lower the heat to low-medium and fry the malpua for about 3–4 minutes on each side, until golden brown on both sides.

Once cooked, remove the malpua carefully from the oil and drain on kitchen paper. Make the rest of the malpuas the same way.

Make sure the sugar syrup is warm (if it's cold, just place the pan of syrup on a low heat to warm it up). Dip the malpuas into the prepared sugar syrup and soak each side for 30 seconds.

Remove from the sugar syrup and place on a serving plate. Garnish with the nuts and serve warm.

> **NOTE**
>
> You can also serve malpuas with chilled rabri (see page 190).

RABRI KULFI

Kulfi is similar to ice cream in appearance but in taste it's more rich and dense. My daughters prefer this to ice cream. You can make it with different flavours, but my favourites are rose and mango. These flavours are very popular in India, too.

1 litre (2 pints) whole milk
3 tablespoons crumbled khoya (dried milk)
100g (3½oz) condensed milk
2 tablespoons coarsely chopped nuts
6–7 green cardamom pods, seeds crushed

Put the whole milk into a heavy-bottomed pan on a medium-high heat. Let it come to the boil, then reduce the heat to medium and simmer for around 30 minutes, stirring it regularly – you don't want the milk to stick to the bottom of the pan. After about 30 minutes, the milk will look quite thick. At this point add the crumbled khoya and the condensed milk. Keep mixing until the khoya and condensed milk have dissolved – this will take 5–7 minutes.

Add the nuts. They will give the kulfi a lot of texture. I cook the milk for around 50–60 minutes in all – it should get really thick by the end and it will continue to thicken as it cools down. Remove the pan from the heat and stir in the crushed cardamom seeds. Leave the mixture to cool down completely.

Once cooled, pour the mixture into kulfi moulds or any other shaped container of your choice. Cover and freeze for about 6–8 hours until completely set.

To serve, hold each kulfi mould under warm running water for 30–45 seconds, then tap the mould on the plate. The kulfi should come out easily. Enjoy!

NOTE

The plus point with making kulfi is that you won't get any ice crystals, because kulfi is made with rabri (reduced milk).

ANJEER KHEER

Kheer is a very traditional Indian dessert made with basic ingredients: rice, milk and sugar. This rice pudding has lots of variations and flavours in India. I have personally tried more than ten different versions, and I'm sharing my personal favourite here.

100g (3½oz) basmati rice
1 teaspoon ghee
1 bay leaf
3–4 green cardamom pods, lightly crushed
1 litre (2 pints) whole milk
100g (3½oz) dried figs, chopped
a few strands of saffron
4–5 tablespoons caster sugar
3 tablespoons chopped nuts (I use chopped cashews and almonds)
1½ teaspoons rose water

Rinse the rice until the water runs clear, then soak it in plenty of cold water for 20–30 minutes. Drain in a colander and set aside.

Heat a heavy-based pan on a medium heat. Add the ghee and the bay leaf and stir for at least 1 minute to infuse the flavour. Add the rice and the crushed cardamom. Toss everything together for 1–2 minutes, stirring constantly, until aromatic.

Add the milk to the pan and stir well. Turn the heat to medium-high and let the milk come to the boil – this will take around 10–12 minutes. Stir regularly so that it doesn't stick to the bottom of the pan. Once the milk has come to the boil, add the chopped figs and saffron and reduce the heat to low. Let the kheer cook for around 25 minutes on a low heat, stirring every 2 minutes or so. The milk will reduce considerably after 25 minutes and the kheer will look thick. The rice will be completely cooked. If you want super thick kheer, cook for a further 15 minutes.

Stir in the sugar and nuts and cook the kheer for 5 more minutes. The sugar should dissolve completely. Don't worry if your kheer doesn't look very thick at this point, it will continue to thicken as it cools down.

Remove the pan from the heat and stir in the rose water. Garnish with more nuts and serve the kheer warm or chilled. I love mine chilled in the refrigerator for 4–5 hours.

CARROT HALWA

This classic Indian dessert never fails to impress. Traditional
Indian halwa is made by simmering carrots in milk and ghee and
is popularly known as gajar ka halwa, gajrela or gajar halwa.
I like to add orange zest to give it a citrus flavour.

15 pistachio nuts
10 whole almonds
10 whole cashews
2 tablespoons ghee
500g (1lb 1½oz) carrots, peeled
   and coarsely grated
1 litre (2 pints) whole milk
a few strands of saffron
200g (7oz) condensed milk
1 tablespoon orange zest
½ teaspoon ground cardamom
150g (5oz) khoya, grated
   (dried milk, optional)

Dry roast the nuts in a small pan on a low heat until lightly golden. Leave to cool, then chop roughly and set aside. Alternatively, you can first chop the nuts, then fry them in 1 tablespoon of the ghee.

Heat the remaining ghee in a large, heavy-based pan and sauté the carrots until all the moisture has evaporated. Add the milk and saffron, bring to the boil and cook on a medium heat for about 15–20 minutes, stirring often, until the milk has completely evaporated. Do not be tempted to leave the pot unattended or the milk will scorch.

Add the condensed milk and orange zest and stir well, then increase the heat and cook until the halwa has been reduced by roughly a third. When it is done, it will have thickened and become aromatic.

Sprinkle over the ground cardamom. If you like, you can add grated khoya at this stage, too. Stir and cook for 2–3 minutes, just until the khoya has blended in well. Garnish with the roasted nuts and serve warm.

PHIRNI

Phirni is a pretty similar dessert to kheer (see page 191), the major difference being that for phirni we use coarse or ground rice but for kheer we use whole rice. I make this dairy-free by using oat milk and cream. In India, phirni is traditionally served chilled in earthenware pots.

50g (1¾oz) basmati rice
1 litre (2 pints) oat milk
100g (3½oz) oat cream
a few strands of saffron
150g (5oz) caster sugar
50g (1¾oz) green raisins
2 tablespoons finely sliced almonds,
    plus more to garnish
½ teaspoon ground green cardamom
1 teaspoon rose water
10 fresh edible rose petals, to garnish

Rinse the rice a couple of times in water, then drain and either let the rice dry on its own or dry it in a kitchen towel.

Blend the rice grains coarsely in a food processor or blender. If you like, you can also soak the rice in water for 30 minutes before blending. Set the ground rice aside.

Heat the milk and cream in a heavy-based pan. When the milk starts to get warm, take 1 tablespoon and place it in a bowl. Stir in the saffron strands and set aside. This will give a nice natural colour and flavour to the rice.

Let the rest of the milk reach a boil. Lower the heat and add the ground rice. Stir and add the sugar. On a low-medium heat, cook the ground rice in the milk for about 15–20 minutes. Do not cover the pan. Keep stirring at regular intervals so that no lumps form and the mixture doesn't stick to the bottom of the pan. When the rice is almost cooked, add the raisins, almonds, cardamom and the saffron dissolved in milk. Stir and cook for a further 5–6 minutes. Once the phirni is ready, add the rose water and set aside to cool down.

Serve warm or chilled, as you prefer. Pour into serving bowls and garnish with almonds and rose petals.

5-COURSE
VEGETARIAN MENU

(1)
Chandni Chowk ki Aloo Tikki
(see page 62)

(2)
Apple and Roots Dhokla Salad
(see page 72)

(3)
Malabar Cauliflower
(see page 77)

(4)
Khubani Soya Keema
(see page 115)

Serve with dal, paratha, rice and raita.

(5)
Phirni
(see page 194)

5-COURSE
VEGAN MENU

(1)
Kidney Bean Kebab
(see page 75)

(2)
Chickpea and Samphire Salad
(see page 61)

(3)
Lotus Root Chilli Fry
(see page 68)

(4)
Mushroom and Truffle Khichadi
(see page 99)

Serve with tadka dal (see page 139),
green mint chutney (see page 172),
jeera aloo (see page 124), *chapati.*

(5)
Poached Pears
(see page 182)

Serve with dairy-free kulfi (see page 190)
or ice cream.

FAMILY CELEBRATION
SHARING MENU

(1)
Chandni Chowk ki Aloo Tikki (see page 62)
Aloo Pyaz Mirch Bhajia (see page 54)
Sun-dried Tomato and Asparagus Rolls (see page 74)
Seasonal Greens Couscous Salad (see page 84)

(2)
Baingan Mirch ka Salan (see page 118)
Palungo ko Saag (see page 141)
Jackfruit Biryani (see page 148)
Punjabi Rajma Rasila (see page 136)
Chur Chur Paratha (see page 164)

(3)
Carrot Halwa (see page 193)
Anjeer Kheer (see page 191)

INDEX

A

aamras poori 185
akuri masala 24
almonds
    carrot halwa 193
    phirni 194
aloo gobi 130
aloo paratha 26
aloo pyaz mirch bhajia 54
aloo tikki
    Chandni Chowk ki aloo tikki 62–3
anjeer kheer 191
apple and roots dhokla salad 72
apricots (dried)
    khubani soya keema 115
    seasonal greens couscous salad 84
arhar/toor dal (yellow lentils)
    tadka dal 139
asafoetida 61
asparagus
    sun-dried tomato and asparagus
        rolls 74
    tawa salad 66
aubergines
    baingan ka bharta 102
    baingan mirch ka salan 118
    bharleli vangi 109
    sambhar 32–3
    vangi bhaat 58–9
avocado chutney 178

B

baingan ka bharta 102
baingan mirch ka salan 118
barfi, rose and cashew 186
beans
    kidney bean kebab 75
    kwati 127
    Punjabi rajma rasila 136
beansprouts
    carrot koshambir 122
    misal pao 35
bedai bhaji 50–1
beetroot
    apple and roots dhokla salad 72
    beetroot cutlets 71
    tawa salad 66
Bengal gram (chana dal)
    dal makhani 131
    kwati 127
berries
    mixed wild berry chutney 173
besan see gram flour
bhaji
    bedai bhaji 50–1
    poori bhaji 47
bharleli vangi 109
bharwan guchhi (stuffed morels) 81
bhature 28–9
bhindi, Jaipuri 126
bhuteko bhat (Nepalese fried rice) 146

B (continued)

biryani
    chickpea and mushroom biryani 161–2
    jackfruit biryani 148–9
black-eyed beans
    kwati 127
black gram, whole
    dal makhani 131
    kwati 127
bottlegourds
    bottlegourd kofta 112
    idli sambhar 32–3
bread
    aamras poori 185
    aloo paratha 26
    bhature 28–9
    bread pakora 44
    chapati 154
    chur chur paratha 164
    makki ki roti 153
    missi roti 152
broccoli
    seasonal greens couscous salad 84
    tawa salad 66
Brussels sprout poriyal 128
butter naan 157

C

cardamom 13
carrots
    beetroot cutlets 71
    carrot halwa 193
    carrot koshambir 122
    sambhar 32–3
    seasonal greens couscous salad 84
    tawa salad 66
    veg tehri (seasonal greens with rice) 160
    vermicelli upma 39
cashews
    carrot halwa 193
    cashew nut paste 19
    gravy 94
    paneer anardana 106
    rose and cashew barfi 186
cauliflower
    aloo gobi 130
    cauliflower pickle 170
    guncho keema 90
    Malabar cauliflower 77
    veg tehri (seasonal greens with rice) 160
celebration sharing menu 201
chana dal (Bengal gram)
    dal makhani 131
    kwati 127
Chandni Chowk ki aloo tikki 62–3
chapati 154
cheese see paneer
Chettinad spice mix 17
chickpea flour see gram flour (besan)
chickpeas
    chickpea and mushroom biryani 161–2
    chickpea and samphire salad 61
    chole bhature 28–9
    kwati 127
    Pindi chana 142
chilla 42
chillies
    chilli/garlic paste 18
    Kashmiri chilli 13
    lotus root chilli fry 68–9
chole bhature 28–9
chur chur paratha 164

C (continued)

chutney
    avocado chutney 178
    coconut chutney 168
    coriander and mint chutney 173
    green mint chutney 172
    mixed wild berry chutney 173
    raw mango chutney 171
    tamarind chutney 176
    tomato chutney 172
    see also pickles
cinnamon 13
cloves 13
coconut
    apple and roots dhokla salad 72
    baingan mirch ka salan 118
    Brussels sprout poriyal 128
    carrot koshambir 122
    chickpea and samphire salad 61
    coconut chutney 168
colour 9
condensed milk
    carrot halwa 193
    rabri kulfi 190
consistency 9
coriander
    avocado chutney 178
    coconut chutney 168
    coriander and mint chutney 173
    green mint chutney 172
coriander seeds 13
courgette mussalam 94
couscous 84
    seasonal greens couscous salad 84
cumin seeds 13
curry
    baingan ka bharta 102
    baingan mirch ka salan 118
    bedai bhaji 50–1
    bharleli vangi 109
    bottlegourd kofta 112
    chole bhature 28–9
    courgette mussalam 94
    curry powder 12
    dum aloo 105
    guncho keema 90
    jackfruit masala 88
    kadai tofu 97
    kadhi pakora 98
    khubani soya keema 115
    lotus root kofta 92–3
    misal pao 35
    mushroom and truffle khichadi 99–100
    paneer anardana 106
    paneer makhani 116
    poori bhaji 47
cutting techniques, julienne 122

D

dal chawal aur achar 80
dal makhani 131
dhokla salad, apple and roots 72
dum aloo 105
dumplings
    bedai bhaji 50–1
    bottlegourd kofta 112
    dal chawal aur achar 80
    lotus root kofta 92–3
    vangi bhaat 58–9

E

eggs
    akuri masala 24

F

family celebration sharing menu 201
figs (dried)
    anjeer kheer 191
flatbreads
    aloo paratha 26
    butter naan 157
    chapati 154
    chur chur paratha 164
    makki ki roti 153
    missi roti 152
French beans
    sun-dried tomato and asparagus
      rolls 74
    tawa salad 66
    veg tehri (seasonal greens with rice) 160
    vermicelli upma 39
fritters
    aloo pyaz mirch bhajia 54
    Jaipuri bhindi 126
    Malabar cauliflower 77
    kadhi pakora 98

G

garam masala 16
garlic
    chilli/garlic paste 18
ghati masala 16
ghee, tempering spices 21
ginger/garlic paste 18
goda masala 17
gram *see* Bengal gram (chana dal);
  black gram
gram flour (besan) 42
    apple and roots dhokla salad 72
    chilla 42
    kadhi pakora 98
    makki ki roti 153
    missi roti 152
gravy
    bottlegourd kofta 112
    courgette mussalam 94
    paneer anardana 106
green mint chutney 172
guncho keema 90

H

halwa, carrot 193
honey
    sweet yoghurt 20

I

idli sambhar 32–3

J

jackfruit
    jackfruit biryani 148–9
    jackfruit masala 88
jaggery 176
    tamarind chutney 176
    zarda (sweet pulao) 156
Jaipuri bhindi 126
jeera aloo 124
julienne cutting technique 122

K

kadai tofu 97
kadhi pakora 98
kalpasi (stone flower) 13
Kashmiri chilli 13
kebab, kidney bean 75
kheer, anjeer 191
khichadi, mushroom and truffle 99–100
khoya (dried milk)
    carrot halwa 193
    courgette mussalam 94
khubani soya keema 115
kidney beans
    kidney bean kebab 75
    kwati 127
    Punjabi rajma rasila 136
koftas
    bottlegourd kofta 112
    lotus root kofta 92–3
kulfi, rabri 190
kwati 127

L

lauki
    bottlegourd kofta 112
lemon dressing 84
lentils
    dal chawal aur achar 80
    dal makhani 131
    kwati 127
    mushroom and truffle khichadi 99–100
    sambhar 32–3
    tadka dal 139
lotus roots
    lotus root chilli fry 68–9
    lotus root kofta 92–3

M

maize flour
    makki ki roti 153
makki ki roti 153
Malabar cauliflower 77
malpua 187
mangetout
    seasonal greens couscous salad 84
mangoes
    aamras poori 185
    raw mango chutney 171
maple syrup
    poached pears 182
menus 196–201

milk

    anjeer kheer 191
    carrot halwa 193
    rabri kulfi 190
    see also khoya (dried milk)
mint
    avocado chutney 178
    coriander and mint chutney 173
    green mint chutney 172
misal pao 35
missi roti 152
mixed wild berry chutney 173
mooli pickle 177
moong beans
    pesarattu 30
morels
    bharwan guchhi (stuffed morels) 81
mushrooms
    bharwan guchhi (stuffed morels) 81
    chickpea and mushroom biryani 161–2
    mushroom and truffle khichadi 99–100
mustard seeds 13

N

naan, butter 157
Nepalese fried rice 146
nuts
    anjeer kheer 191
    see also almonds; cashews etc

O

oat milk
    phirni 194
oil, tempering spices 21
okra
    Jaipuri bhindi 126
onions
    akuri masala 24
    aloo pyaz mirch bhajia 54
    baingan ka bharta 102
    bharleli vangi 109
    bottlegourd kofta 112
    Brussels sprout poriyal 128
    chickpea and mushroom biryani 161–2
    chole bhature 28–9
    fried onions 21
    jackfruit masala 88
    kadai tofu 97
    khubani soya keema 115
    kwati 127
    lotus root kofta 92–3
    misal pao 35
    mushroom and truffle khichadi 99–100
    onion paste 21
    palak paneer 134
    palungo ko saag 141
    paneer anardana 106
    paneer bhurji 138
    poha masala 46
    Punjabi rajma rasila 136
    tadka dal 139
    veg tehri (seasonal greens with rice) 160

P

pakoras
aloo pyaz mirch bhajia 54
bread pakora 44
kadhi pakora 98
palak paneer 134
palungo ko saag 141
pancakes
chilla 42
malpua 187
pesarattu 30
paneer
palak paneer 134
paneer anardana 106
paneer bhurji 138
paneer makhani 116
stuffed sweet peppers 64
parathas
aloo paratha 26
chur chur paratha 164
peanuts
baingan mirch ka salan 118
beetroot cutlets 71
bharleli vangi 109
carrot koshambir 122
sabudana khichdi 43
pears, poached 182
peas
baingan ka bharta 102
poha masala 46
Punjabi samosa 36–7
sun-dried tomato and asparagus
rolls 74
tofu and green pea tikki 82
veg tehri (seasonal greens with rice)
160
peas (dried)
Chandni Chowk ki aloo tikki 62–3
kwati 127
peas, yellow split see toor dal
peppers
guncho keema 90
kadai tofu 97
paneer bhurji 138
stuffed sweet peppers 64
pesarattu 30
phirni 194
pickles
cauliflower pickle 170
mooli pickle 177
see also chutney
Pindi chana 142
pistachio nuts
carrot halwa 193
poha masala 46
pooris
aamras poori 185
bedai bhaji 50–1
poori bhaji 47
poriyal, Brussels sprout 128
potatoes
aloo gobi 130
aloo paratha 26
aloo pyaz mirch bhajia 54
bedai bhaji 50–1
beetroot cutlets 71
bread pakora 44
Chandni Chowk ki aloo tikki 62–3
courgette mussalam 94
dum aloo 105
jeera aloo 124
kidney bean kebab 75
lotus root kofta 92–3

poha masala 46
poori bhaji 47
Punjabi samosa 36–7
sabudana khichdi 43
stuffed sweet peppers 64
sun-dried tomato and asparagus
rolls 74
tareko aloo (crispy fried potatoes) 56
veg tehri (seasonal greens with rice) 160
pulao
zarda (sweet pulao) 156
pumpkin
sambhar 32–3
Punjabi rajma rasila 136
Punjabi samosa 36–7

R

rabri kulfi 190
radishes
mooli pickle 177
raisins
phirni 194
raw mango chutney 171
rice
anjeer kheer 191
bhuteko bhat (Nepalese fried rice) 146
chickpea and mushroom biryani 161–2
dal chawal aur achar 80
idli sambhar 32–3
jackfruit biryani 148–9
mushroom and truffle khichadi 99–100
pesarattu 30
phirni 194
poha masala 46
vangi bhaat 58–9
veg tehri (seasonal greens with rice) 160
zarda (sweet pulao) 156
rose water
phirni 194
rose and cashew barfi 186
rotis
makki ki roti 153
missi roti 152

S

sabudana khichdi 43
saffron
carrot halwa 193
phirni 194
zarda (sweet pulao) 156
salads
apple and roots dhokla salad 72
carrot koshambir 122
chickpea and samphire salad 61
seasonal greens couscous salad 84
tawa salad 66
salt, spiced 20
sambhar 32–3
samosa, Punjabi 36–7
samphire
chickpea and samphire salad 61
seasonal greens couscous salad 84
sesame seeds
baingan mirch ka salan 118
side dishes
aloo gobi 130
Brussels sprout poriyal 128
carrot koshambir 122
dal makhani 131

Jaipuri bhindi 126
jeera aloo 124
kwati 127
palak paneer 134
palungo ko saag 141
paneer bhurji 138
Pindi chana 142
Punjabi rajma rasila 136
tadka dal 139
single thread consistency, sugar syrup 186
soya beans
kwati 127
soya mince
khubani soya keema 115
spiced salt 20
spices 11–21
pastes 18–19
spice blends 16–17
tempering spices 21
spinach
palak paneer 134
palungo ko saag 141
spring roll wrappers
sun-dried tomato and asparagus
rolls 74
star anise 13
stone flower (kalpasi) 13
sugar syrup
malpua 187
single thread consistency 186
sun-dried tomato and asparagus rolls 74
sweet yoghurt 20

T

tadka
idli sambhar 32–3
kadhi pakora 98
tadka dahi 80
tadka dal 139
tamarind
tamarind chutney 176
tamarind paste 35
tapioca
sabudana khichdi 43
tareko aloo (crispy fried potatoes) 56
tawa salad 66
tea
chole bhature 28–9
Pindi chana 142
tempering spices 21
texture 9
tikkis (patties)
Chandni Chowk ki aloo tikki 62–3
tofu and green pea tikki 82
tofu
kadai tofu 97
tofu and green pea tikki 82
tomatoes
akuri masala 24
aloo gobi 130
baingan ka bharta 102
bharleli vangi 109
chickpea and mushroom biryani 161–2
guncho keema 90
jackfruit masala 88
kadai tofu 97
khubani soya keema 115
lotus root kofta 92–3
mushroom and truffle khichadi 99–100
palak paneer 134
palungo ko saag 141
paneer anardana 106

paneer makhani 116
Punjabi rajma rasila 136
sun-dried tomato and asparagus
  rolls 74
tadka dal 139
tomato chutney 172
veg tehri (seasonal greens with rice) 160
toor dal (yellow lentils)
dal chawal aur achar 80
mushroom and truffle khichadi 99–100
sambhar 32–3
truffles
mushroom and truffle khichadi 99–100
turmeric 13

U

urad dal
idli sambhar 32–3

V

vangi bhaat 58–9
veg tehri (seasonal greens with rice) 160
vegan menu 198
vegetables
see also peppers, spinach etc
vegetarian menu 196
vermicelli upma 39

Y

yoghurt
apple and roots dhokla salad 72
dum aloo 105
kadhi pakora 98
sweet yoghurt 20
tadka dahi 80

Z

zarda (sweet pulao) 156

UK/US GLOSSARY

UK	US
aubergine	eggplant
baking parchment	parchment paper
baking tray	baking sheet
beetroot	beet
bicarbonate of soda	baking soda
black-eye beans	black eyed peas
caster sugar	superfine sugar
chickpeas	garbanzo beans
chilli/chillies	chili/chiles
chilli flake	red pepper flakes
coriander	cilantro
cornflour	cornstarch
courgettes	zucchini
desiccated coconut	shredded coconut
double cream	heavy cream
flour: plain, wholemeal	all-purpose, whole wheat
frying pan	skillet
griddle pan	grill pan
grill/grilling	broiler/broiling
kitchen foil	aluminum foil
kitchen paper	paper towels
mangetout	snow peas
natural yogurt	plain yogurt
pepper	bell pepper
salad leaves	salad greens
single cream	pouring cream
(oven) shelf	(oven) rack
sieve	strainer
spring onion	scallion
starter	appetizer
stone	pit
tin	pan

INGREDIENTS GLOSSARY

Ajwain seed	carom seeds
Aloo	potatoes
Aloo bhujia	Indian snacks made with potato and gram flour
Amchur	dried mango powder
Amla	dried gooseberries
Besan	gram (chickpea) flour
Bhature	deep-fried fermented bread
Black salt	rock salt from the Himalayan region, with a pungent, sulphurous smell
Chana dal	split chickpeas
Ghee	clarified butter
Idli	southern Indian rice cakes
Idli rice	parboiled rice, used for making idli and dosa
Jaggery	coarse dark brown sugar made from palm tree sap
Kadai	Indian circular cooking pan, similar to a wok
Kalpasi	black stone flower, a species of lichen used as a spice in southern India
Kamal kakdi	lotus root
Kasundi	fermented mustard sauce
Kasuri Methi	dried fenugreek leaves
Kathi rolls	street-food dish from West Bengal, a filling wrapped inside a flatbread
Kewra water	extract of pandanus flowers, used in northern Indian cooking
Khoya	dried milk powder, used in desserts
Lachha onion	raw sliced onion salad with spices
Lauki	bottlegourd
Masoor dal	red lentils
Panch phoron	spice mix used in eastern India and Bangladesh, consisting of cumin seeds, mustard seeds, fenugreek, nigella seeds and fennel seeds
Paratha	Indian flatbread
Poha	pressed rice
Pomegranate powder	dehydrated pomegranate juice
Poori	deep-fried bread
Rajma	kidney beans
Saag	spinach
Sahi jeera	black cumin seeds
Sambhar powder	a spice mix made with cumin seeds, coriander seeds, fenugreek and chillies
Sooji	semolina
Soondha namak	rock salt
Tadka	tempering: frying spices quickly in oil to pour over a finished dish
Tawa	griddle
Tej patta	Indian bay leaf, Cinnamomum tamala; different in flavour from European bay leaves
Thali	large serving dish; also a group of dishes served together
Toor dal	yellow split peas
Urad dal	split black gram

THANK YOU NOTE

I would like to thank a few people, without whom this book would have not been completed.

I am very grateful to Judith Hannam, Publishing Director of Kyle, for believing in me. My special thanks to my editor Louise McKeever, who supported me during the whole journey of my first book and also to my photographer Maja and her entire team who worked very hard in producing perfect clicks and my designers at Evi-O. Thank you to my agent, Heather. They have all been an amazing support and helped me a lot in the completion of TARKARI.

Finally, I am blessed to have such a supportive family and am grateful to my wife Akansha and my daughters (Trisha and Tanisha) who have been a great support and have not complained about my busy schedule. They have always encouraged me to give my best. Due to lockdown, I tried lots of dishes at home and my daughters were difficult critics to please.

ABOUT THE AUTHOR

Michelin-starred Rohit Ghai has become one of the culinary world's most in-demand chefs after a hugely successful decade on the London restaurant scene.

His first solo restaurant, Kutir, opened its doors in late 2018 to rave reviews. Chef Ghai also launched a street-food diner, KoolCha, at Wembley's BOXPARK in early 2019. His third restaurant, with a fine-dining concept, will open in late 2021.

Chef Ghai's precise cooking techniques and innovative dishes have won him praise from celebrities, dignitaries and some of the nation's most discerning food critics. He has also made TV appearances on shows such as the BBC's *MasterChef*, Channel 4, Sony TV and Zee TV.